Copyright © 2019 Ami Sarasvati. All rights reserved.

3rd Edition.

Special thanks to:
My NAF teachers; Clint Goss and Vera Shanov for their fabulous Native American Flute workshops; my beloved children Justin and Rose who inspire me with their courage, tenacity, and love; my Mom and Dad who helped create the foundation for my musical career; Concord Hospital (Concord, NH) for the remarkable experiences as a Certified Music Practitioner; the flute makers who have made many beautiful flutes for me and my students including JP Gomez (Heartsong Flutes), Kuzin Bruce Belmore, Rich Dubé (Northern Spirit Flutes), Odell Borg (High Spirits Flutes), Bob White Bear, the late Stephen DeRuby, Kai Mayberger, and others. Thank you to the trees for giving of themselves so that we may have these wonderful instruments. Thank you to all my students, in-person and online, and of course the Wild Kachinas—you ladies know who you are!

Transcribed in Nakai Flute Tablature courtesy of R. Carlos Nakai

Fingercharts courtesy of Clint Goss   www.NAFTracks.com

Edited by Pam LaCroix of Your Own Words: www.yourownwords.biz

Logo, cover flute, and Kachinas created by Susan Englert: www.becreativesc.com

Book design by Ami Sarasvati

Cover design by Christos Angelidakis

Native American flute arrangements by Ami Sarasvati

Get Your Free Gifts Now!

As a heartfelt thank you, I've created downloads to support your learning.

For your free gifts, go to
www.LearnToPlayNAF.com

Welcome

Each journey with the Native American style flute (NAF) is unique and enchanting. Everyone learns at their own pace and there are many paths to becoming a "good" NAF player. We have been playing flutes for thousands of years. In essence, we reunite with our ancestors by playing the native flute. This instrument is 100% natural and requires no tuning. The transcendent quality of its gorgeous tones gifts us each time we play. A *new musical voice* is accessed through our breath, and then through our flute. This simple and ancient instrument gives us a voice that is soothing, harmonious, and healing. Additionally, each flute has its own secrets and personality.

Having grown up playing classical piano, I truly appreciate the simplicity and portability of the Native American style flute. I also treasure how much fun it is to play with others, inside or outdoors. Truly, the Native American style flute put the "play" factor back into my musical life!

With a moderate amount of dedication, you can learn to play the NAF within a few months. Live instruction, privately or in a group, accelerates your learning and helps you to avoid developing bad habits. With this course under your belt, you will be well on your way to happily playing NAF for a lifetime. I invite you to be gentle with yourself. Allow your hands, body, and ears to get to know how it *feels* and *sounds* to play your flute.

Playing the flute requires breathing fully and frequently. This type of deep breathing renews our energy even when we play for a few minutes. Playing the Native American style flute is a healing art and is a source of comfort to the player as well as the listeners. May your flute bring you countless moments of joy and harmony.

Welcome to a beautiful journey,

Ami Sarasvati

Discover Your Heartsong

Discovering and expressing our emotions through the flute can be cathartic. The gentle tones can help us experience and release our feelings ranging from pure elation to deep pain. The NAF gives us a voice to explore and discover our heartsong.

The flute makes no judgment. It does not buy into any story, but instead offers a way to express and heal what is. In this inner landscape of discovering one's heartsong, the mask is off, perhaps eyes are closed, and Spirit sings through the flute. In these moments of truth, we have the choice to connect within, feel, and transcend.

As we embark on the journey with the NAF, know that this instrument was originally used as a courting flute. The history of the flute was nearly completely lost around 1900. It was through the dedicated efforts of a few songkeepers that we can enjoy the lure of the NAF and its renaissance today.

In times past, a man, hoping to win the love of the lady who has captured his heart, would court her by playing his flute. In the tepee village, since they were not allowed to be together after dark, he could play his heartsong to her within earshot so she would hear him and know of his longing to be with her. This is the story of the Native American style flute giving voice to the energies of passion, creativity, raw emotion, joy, and sorrow. The NAF is a powerful instrument and it is said that after winning her heart, the man would put the flute away. At the time of his death, the flute may have been buried along with his body.

We pick up our flute and take a deep breath in. In the space between silence and the voice of the flute, the heart searches for an opening. For a moment, our heartsong is literally suspended in thin air. It manifests and then vanishes forever. Spirit plays through the union of breath and flute. Come celebrate this musical mystery by discovering your own heartsong.

Flute playing is an ever-present invitation to discover your heartsong.

Checklist

You will need:
- a well tuned six-hole Native American style flute. If you have a five-hole flute, simply disregard the instruction regarding keeping the third hole from the top covered, as a five-hole flute does not have this hole.
- this book.
- if you are taking lessons online, a high speed connection, webcam, and microphone.
- a great desire to learn to play the Native American style flute.
- a sense of ADVENTURE!

Recommendations:
- Obtain a simple metronome or metronome app on a smart phone or device.
- Set up a dedicated place to keep your flute out where it is easily accessible.
  NOTE: If you have animals, be sure your flute is kept somewhere out of reach. I learned the hard way when my dog literally ate my first flute after I left it out where she could get at it.
- At the beginning, practice in front of a mirror as often as possible until the squeaking stops.
- Remember to *touch* your flute(s) every day.
- Consider purchasing my Student NAF CD "One Life" available on Amazon.
- Take advantage of the many videos mentioned throughout this book. They are meant to augment your learning as only video or live instruction can.

IMPORTANT: Check your block alignment when you first pick up a flute to play.

You can instantly recognize an experienced NAF player when you see them FIRST check the block placement when they pick up the flute. Be sure to make this a habit.

See how the block is out of line?   *This block is lined up nicely.*

Native American Flute Anatomy

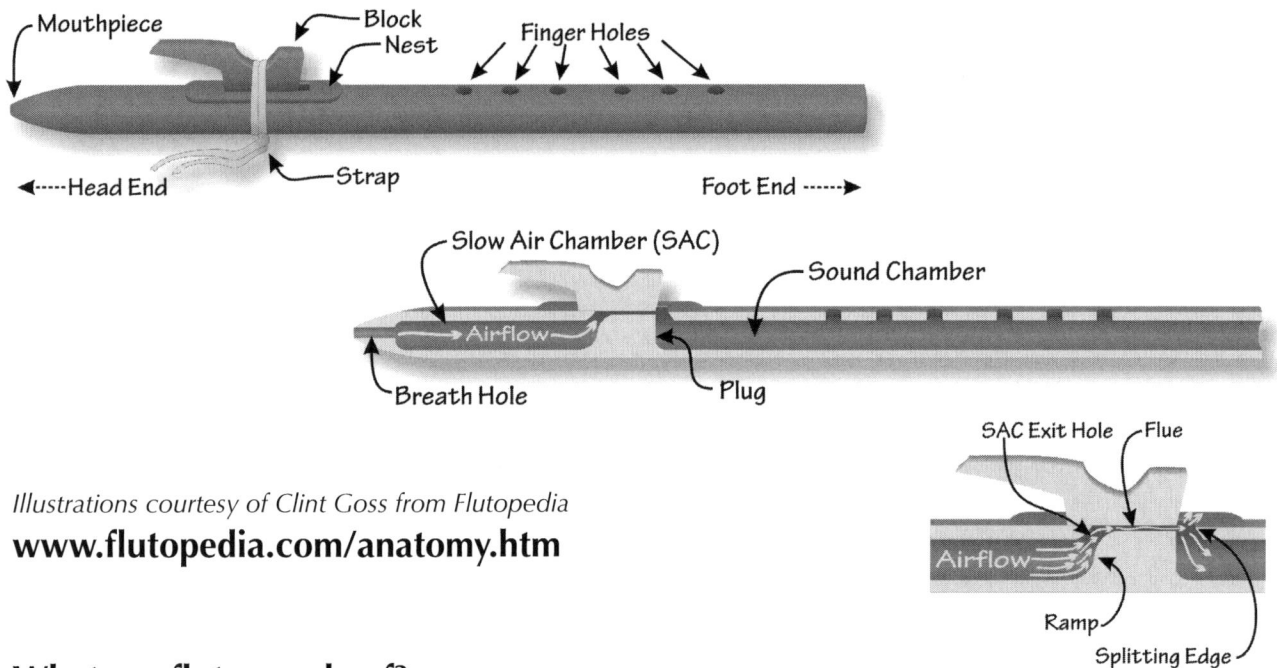

Illustrations courtesy of Clint Goss from Flutopedia
www.flutopedia.com/anatomy.htm

What are flutes made of?
Flutes are made of different woods and plastics. Each offers its own unique sound and tone.

The purpose of the leather strapping:
The strapping keeps the block in the right place on the flute for good tone. It often loosens and should be checked often for tightness. It should be tied down tightly securing the block in place.

Wetting out happens.
After about 20-30 minutes of continuous play, your flute may wet out. Do your best to transfer as little moisture as possible into your flute as you play. Hold your flute at a 45 degree angle in front of you as you play to minimize saliva runoff which occurs when your mouth is pointed down onto the flute. This happens if the flute is held too close to your body. Allow it to float in front of you.

If your flute wets out and no longer plays, you can leave it to dry (ideally upside down) for several hours or untie the leather strapping, remove the block, dry the flue using a clean napkin or paper towel, re-strap the block onto the flute, realign the block perfectly, and resume playing.

Note: in the cold weather, playing your flute outside will cause it to wet out even sooner.

Protect your flute.
When not playing your flute, keep it out of direct sunlight and away from anywhere it could be harmed by weather, animals, or other potential risks.

To share or not to share?
Germs can be transferred by mouth contact on your flute. Use common sense.

Body Awareness and Postures for Best Results

Block "posture"

Check the block (also called the bird, fetish, totem, or other names) each time before you play:
- Be sure the block is aligned properly and is tied down very well for good tonal quality.

Finger "posture"

Correct finger posture:
- Relax your hands.
- Practice playing imaginary finger cymbals to train your fingers not to put fingertips into holes.
- Allow your fingers to be nearly flat on the holes of your flute.
- Bend primarily at the third knuckle.
- Keep your pinkie fingers relaxed (not curled up and tense) and in front of the flute as you play.
- Allow the flute to float in front of you.

Body "posture"

How to hold the flute:
- Hold the flute about 45 degrees away from your waist; let it *float* there.
- Relax your shoulders.
- Avoid hunching down over your flute.
- Let your lungs and heart open.
- Elbows are relaxed and pointed down and slightly in front of your waist.
- Relax, relax, relax your body.
- Your hands will become increasingly relaxed over time.

Lip "posture" or position

The embouchure:
- Pucker gently and *slightly* open your lips.
- Rest your flute on the bottom lip which is pulled back slightly against the lower teeth.
- Avoid putting the flute into your mouth otherwise you'll wet out your flute in no time.
- This is worth repeating: **Do not encircle flute in your mouth.**

Belly breathing

When you practice in front of the mirror, notice if your shoulders are going up and down. Keep your shoulders relaxed and low and breathe from the diaphragm.

10 Hours

The Challenge: the First 10 hours

You will be amazed what is on the other side of your first ten hours of playing!

Practice in 10 to 15 minute intervals with the initial goal of getting the first ten hours under your belt in a few weeks.

Mirror practice

Mirror practice is a recommendation that cannot be over emphasized at the beginning of your NAF playing. It will instantly "show" you why you are squeaking by revealing visually which holes are not fully covered.

Mirror practice is the fastest way to stop squeaking. Squeaking happens because one or more holes is not **100% covered**. Period. Usually, the flute is not the problem.

Learn to wiggle your fingers into the holes when you hear squeaking. Try not to pick your hand up completely off the hole. Just wiggle in and feel the entire circle of the hole under your flattened finger pad.

If squeaking persists, practice with long tones on each note and feel the bottom edge of the holes under your fingers.

The Pentatonic Scale

Remember, this scale is played starting with all the holes covered and moving up, opening one hole at a time. The ring finger of the top hand is always held down for this scale. Practice slowly aiming for good quality tones. Take one breath and play one note. Repeat this a few times, then move up to the next note.

Once you get comfortable, try two or three notes per breath. Practice going up and down the scale. Ideally, practice in front of a mirror as much as possible during your first week so you can immediately see where there are gaps in finger coverage over the holes.

You are now seeing the flute diagrams also represented using Nakai Tablature which you will learn about later in this book.

Going up the Pentatonic Scale

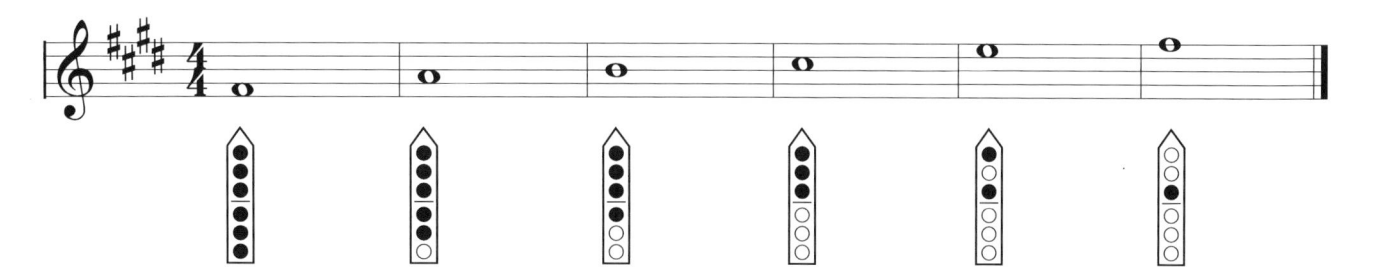

Play the pentatonic scale three times going from the bottom up.

Going down the Pentatonic Scale

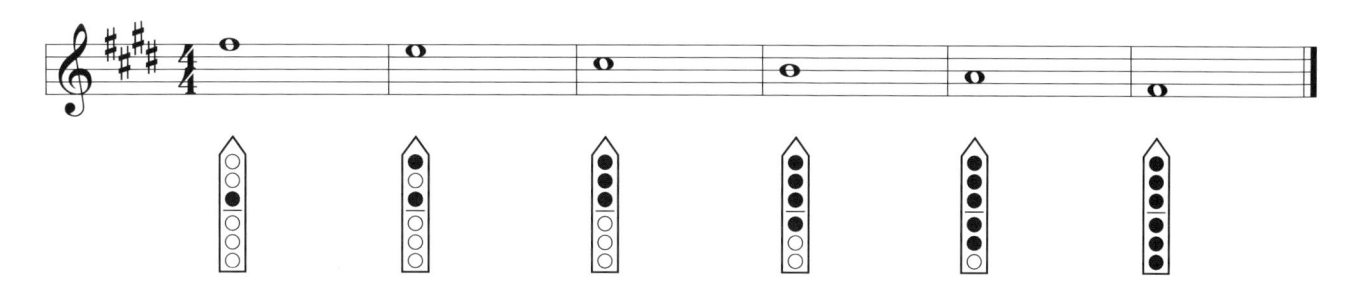

Now, play the pentatonic scale three times going from the top down.

Believe it or not, you already have quite a bit to work with to play your NAF. Before going any further, watch this video by Clint Goss which will help you integrate the concepts we've covered:
https://youtu.be/Uv9Tw8RwY5Y

The Pentatonic Scale, Climbing the Ladder

Notice the ladder below. It has six rungs. Now imagine climbing it. You start on the bottom and work your way up, one rung at a time. As you descend the ladder, you start at the top and climb down one rung at a time. You have six levels to be on. You are not working with a combination of steps, but specifically a straight line working up from the bottom.

This analogy applies exactly to the first scale you will learn on your NAF flute, the pentatonic minor. You don't need to be concerned if you don't know what that means. It is just the basic scale of the NAF. Traditionally, there were only five holes on the flutes (and still many five-hole flutes are out there). Your six-hole flute has the capability of playing a variety of scales which is why it is nice to have a six-hole flute for more variety down the road. Now, we will start with the pentatonic minor and consider the concept of the ladder. Keep it simple and slow as you absorb this and you can learn the finger positions of this scale before you finish reading this page.

Simply start with the all holes covered and exhale gently into your flute until the end of the breath. Now lift the bottom finger and play that note with a long breath. Keep going, one "rung" at a time. **Remember that for your six-hole NAF, you will always hold down your top hand's ring finger.** Imagine your flute is this ladder. Slowly go up and down the scale to get a feel for what the six notes are that you will be working with first.

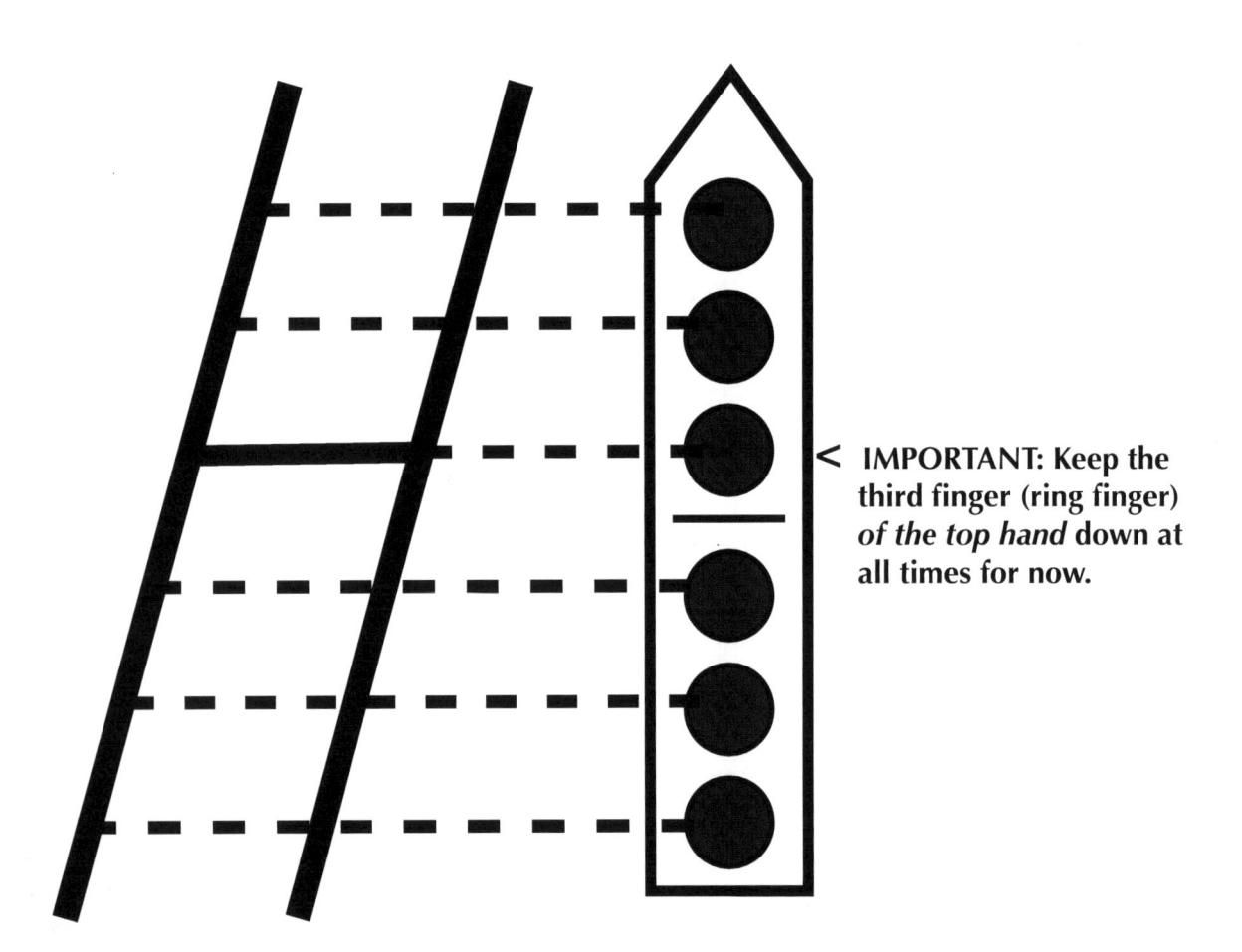

< **IMPORTANT: Keep the third finger (ring finger)** *of the top hand* **down at all times for now.**

Long Tones

Beginning your training on the NAF with long tones sets the foundation for good quality tones. Release any need for speed at this point on your journey. It is fundamental to first learn how each note sounds and feels. Keep in mind the bottom note is the most challenging note to play and often tricky for the beginner. Just about every NAF player faces this challenge. Hang in there! Your fingers will figure this out quickly and you'll be happy you persisted. Do your best to keep your fingers flat and your hands relaxed. Allow the fingertips, especially your middle fingers of each hand, to overlap your flute.

If the tone does not sound pure, wiggle your fingers into the holes. Feel the bottom edge of each hole. Avoid lifting the fingers up to fix; just wiggle them in and play flat-fingered. Go to **https://soundcloud.com/ami-sarasvati**. Select **Playlists**. Scroll down to **Level 1 Student Recordings**. See **Long Tones**. Play along on the appropriate flute (A or G) and try to match each tone, aiming for a pure sound.

- Start on the bottom note.
- Remember to use a very soft breath on this note.
- Play three times using one long breath each time.
- Try varying your breath volume and observe the tone.

- Lift the bottom finger.
- Play three times using one long breath each time.
- Try varying your breath volume and observe the tone.

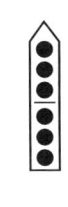

Overblowing the bottom note:
Most beginners initially struggle with this. The bottom note requires a very light breath. The tone quickly jumps to the octave with even the slightest extra breath. This is called overblowing. Simply reduce the volume of breath used on the bottom note to get a nice, low, pure sound.

- Play with the top four holes covered.
- Play three times using one long breath each time.
- Try varying your breath volume and observe the tone.

- Play with the top three holes covered.
- Play three times using one long breath each time.
- Try varying your breath volume and observe the tone.

- Keep your ring finger down on the top hand and play the next note up.
- Play three times using one long breath each time.
- Try varying your breath volume and observe the tone.

- Play the top note (the octave).
- Give this one a lot of breath.
- Play three times using one long breath each time.

What does the Octave refer to?
The tone of the bottom note is found again, at a higher pitch, on the top note of the minor pentatonic scale. To our ear, the octave is the resolution of the interval sequence of the scale.

Neighboring Notes

Playing neighboring notes will help you get comfortable with getting to know this scale. We will start by playing two notes, back and forth, exploring the interval, the position of the fingers, and hearing the tones each note produces. Playing very slowly will yield fast results, so please practice as if in slow motion as you work with this concept on your flute.

Play these two notes back and forth for at least a few minutes. Aim for good tonal quality.

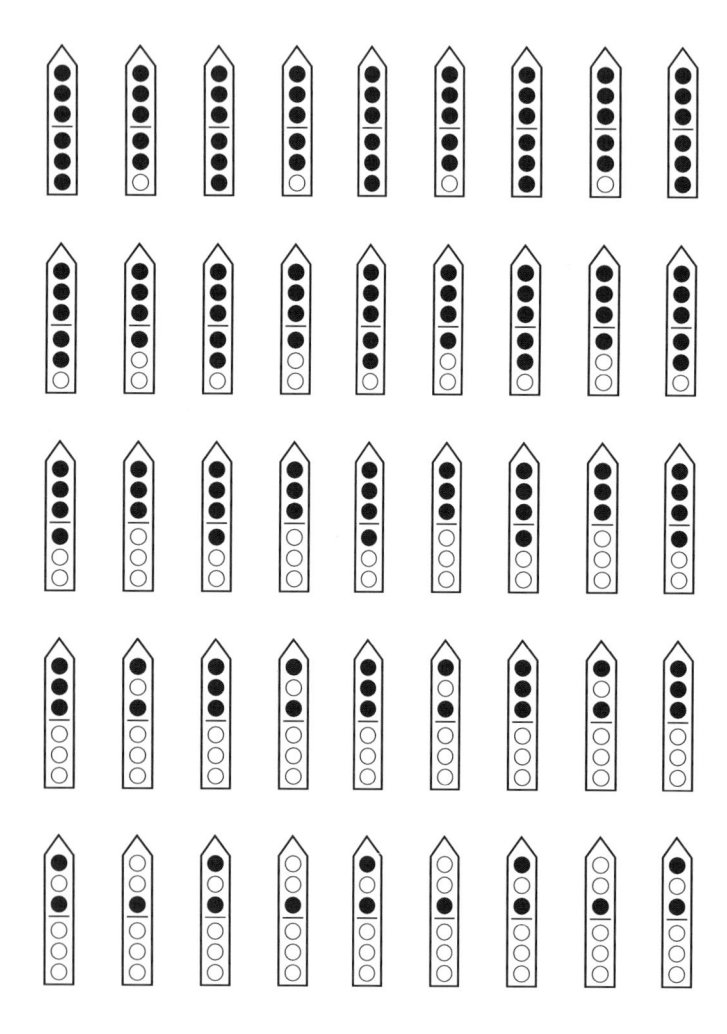

Hold this last note all the way to the end of the breath.

Now start at the top note and descend in the same manner.

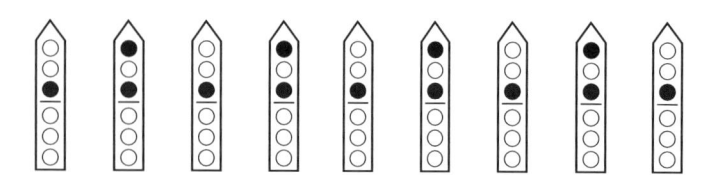

Continue the pattern down to the bottom note.

Improvising on Neighboring Notes

Next, we embark on the journey of improvisation. The NAF is a simple instrument and the beginner is initially working with only six notes. Imagine a piano with 88 keys. The idea of improvisation could be daunting. With the NAF, initial improvisation is accessible if we simply stay on the ladder of the pentatonic minor scale. A harmonious sequence will always be the result due to the beauty and simplicity of this scale. By using both short and long notes, a song begins to form. Adding articulation and ornaments will further color your playing. Let's start with the basic idea for now.

Here are three beginning sequences to get started on a improvisational exploration.

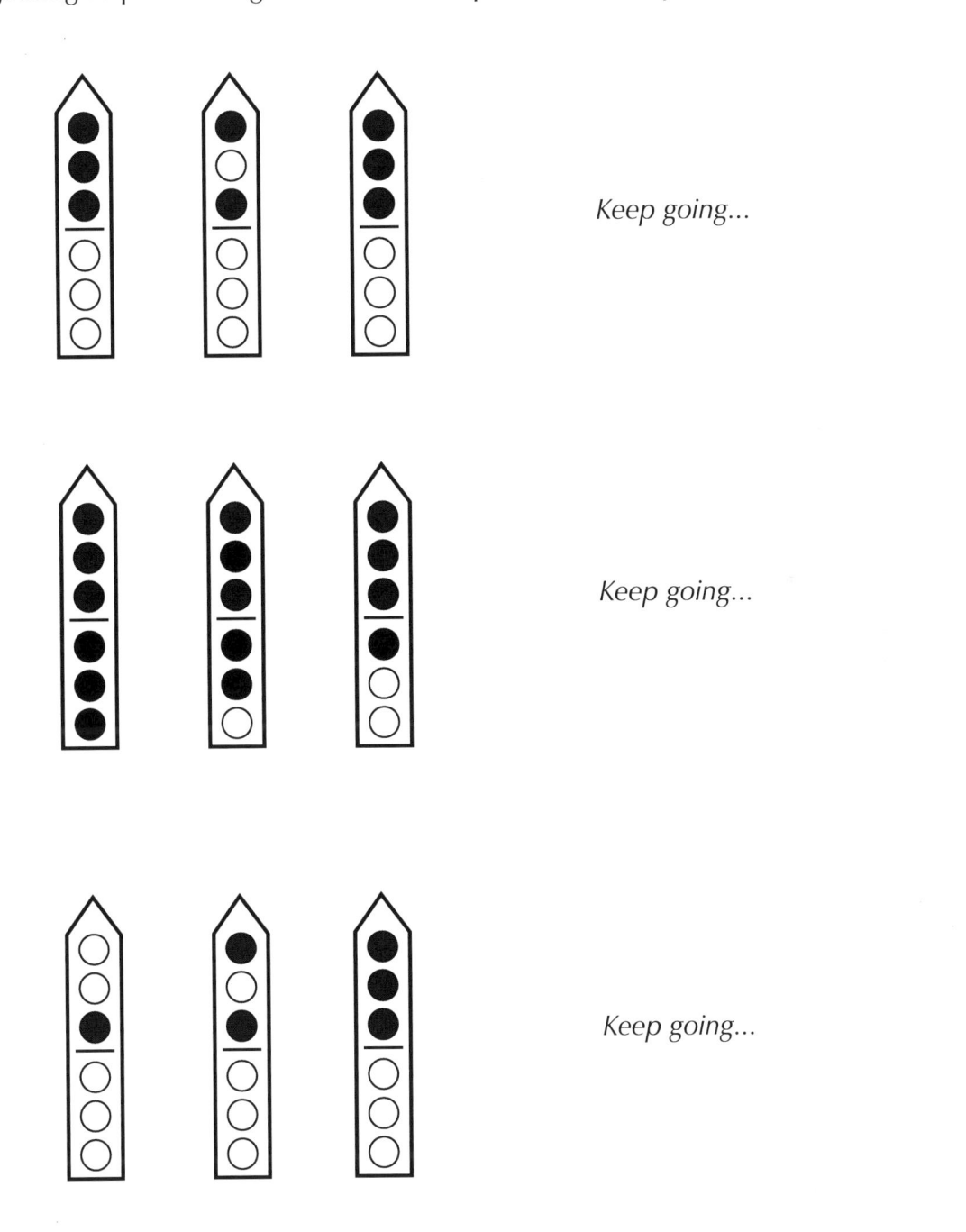

Keep going...

Keep going...

Keep going...

Improvising on Neighboring Notes, continued

Watch this concept on YouTube.
The Scale Song by Clint Goss: **https://youtu.be/Uv9Tw8RwY5Y**

Here are several possible beginnings to an improvisational journey, just using neighboring notes. Keep in mind, for now, simply play notes that are next to each other. You can go up or you can go down, but for this exercise, only play notes that are neighbors, in either direction. Start to ride your breath as you explore different sequences. Play as long as you like and see where this musical journey takes you. Welcome in space between phrases and breaths. Let the tones integrate in the silence and peace.

~   This symbol signifies holding the note for an additional beat.

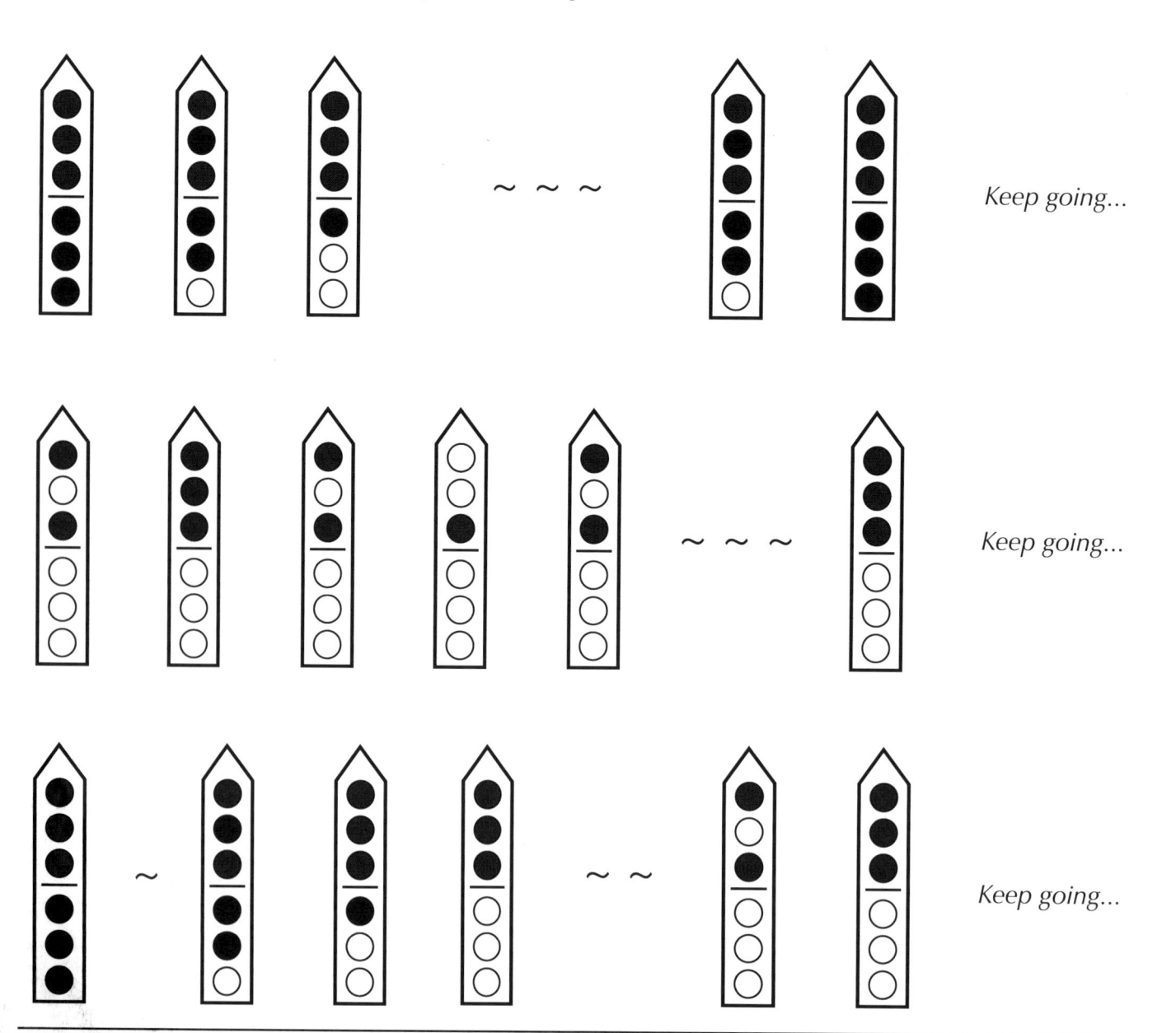

Keep going...

Keep going...

Keep going...

Jumps (or Leaps)

The next step on this journey brings us to "jumps" or "leaps" on your NAF. Instead of playing neighboring notes, you will now be able to go from whatever note you were on to any other note. The rules of the game are that you stay on the notes of the pentatonic minor scale. As mentioned before, there are many other scales that this flute is capable of playing. With the purpose of mastering the pentatonic minor though, we are going to stay on the notes that we've covered so far. Here are a few examples of jumps:

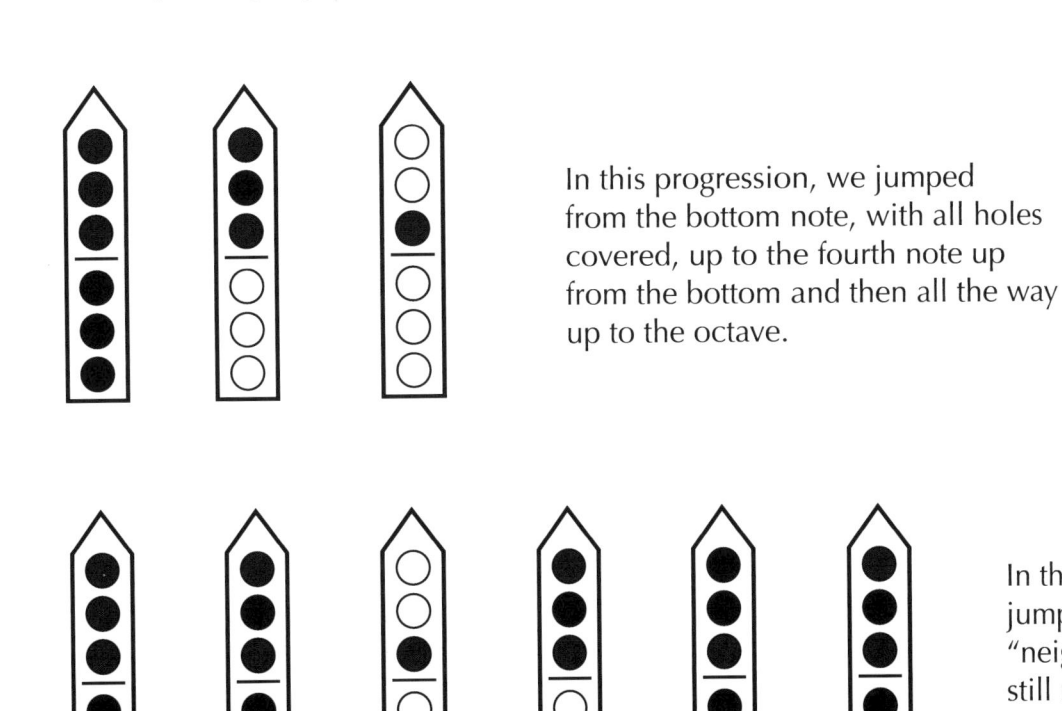

In this progression, we jumped from the bottom note, with all holes covered, up to the fourth note up from the bottom and then all the way up to the octave.

In this progression again, we jumped to notes that are not "neighbors" but that are all still notes on the pentatonic minor scale.

Use the flute diagrams below and color in the holes to make a progression of jumps. As you can see, the fourth hole up is always covered in this scale. Stay on the pentatonic scale.

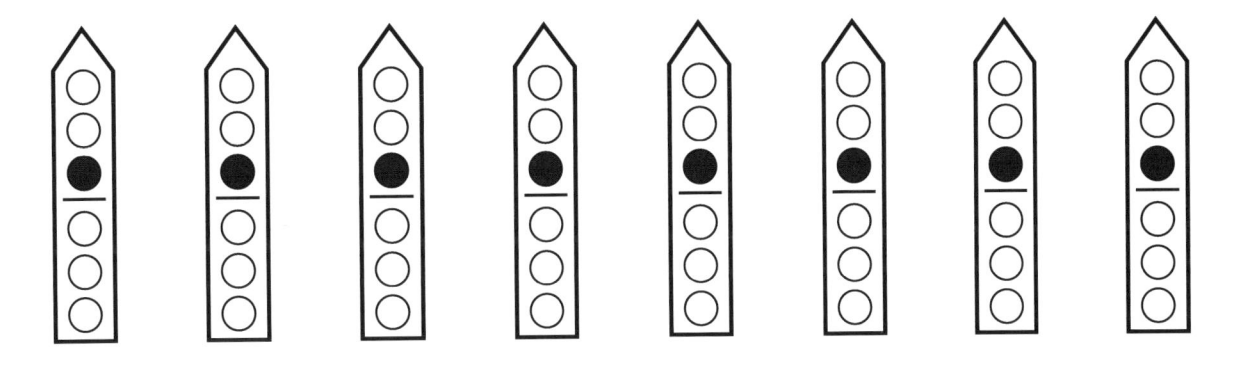

Neighboring Notes and Jumps on the Pentatonic Minor Scale

Next, let's apply these two concepts and begin improvising on the flute. Be relaxed in your timing and just allow yourself to explore how long you'd like to hold each note. Here is a loose interpretation of timing. Neighboring notes and jumps are used in each of these examples.

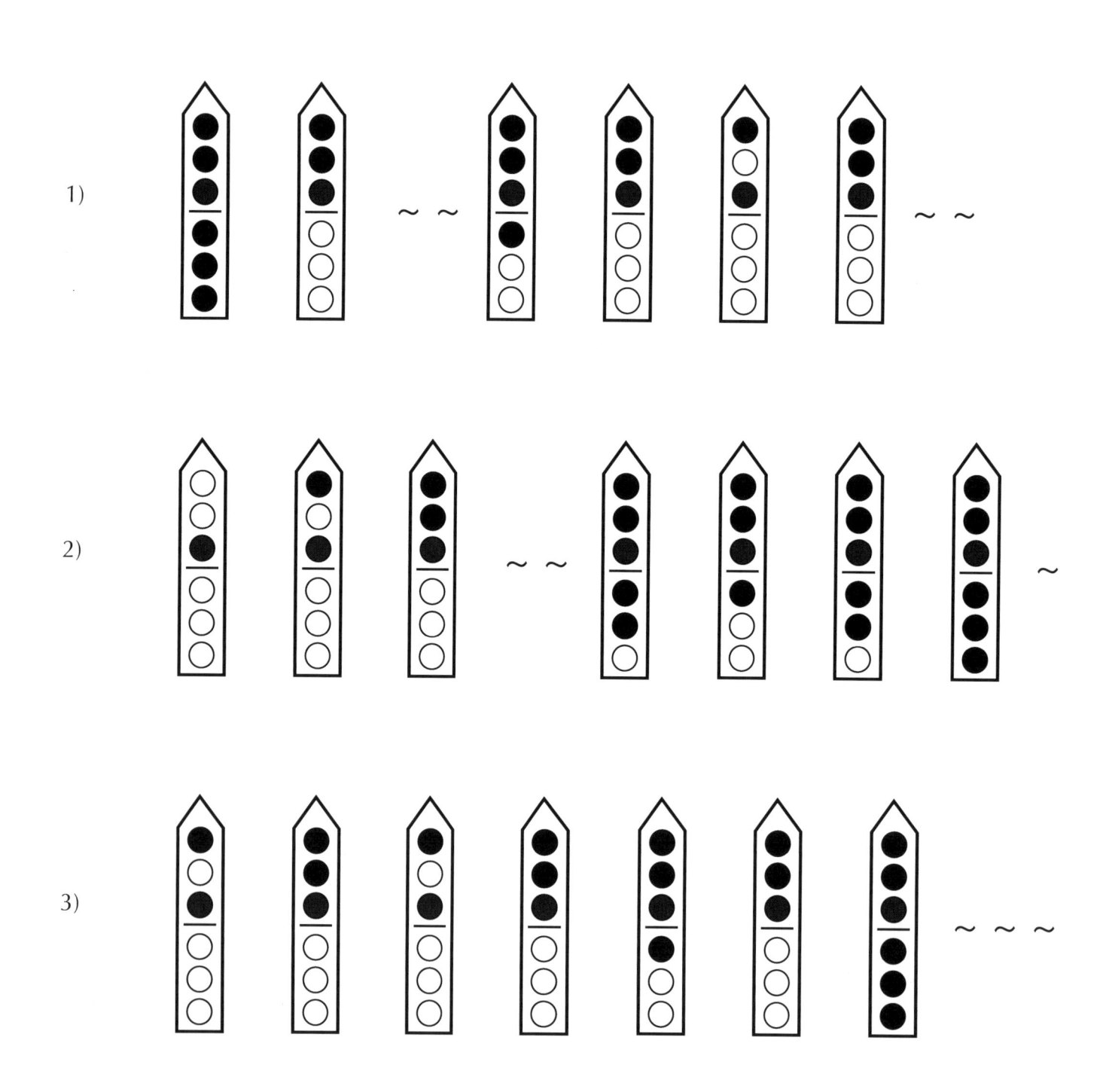

1)

2)

3)

Playing from the Heart

Playing from the heart is the alpha and the omega of the Native American style flute. Although we can learn to play well-known songs that have been written down in order to be rehearsed and memorized, native flute players of years past did not use written music.

The NAF is easy to learn to play and is ideal as an instrument for self expression, especially when we play it from the heart. With each breath, we can tune into our emotions and express longing, joy, grief, and creativity.

Playing from the heart and getting in touch with our emotions, takes courage. In Virginia Woolf's book, *A Room of One's Own*, she breathes literary life into a moment of pure exploration. Woolf captures her character's moment of mystery, "She will light a torch in that vast chamber where nobody has yet been. It is all half lights and profound shadows like those serpentine caves where one goes with a candle, peering up and down, not knowing where one is stepping."

As we open up to our heart, it can be unfamiliar territory, yet it is a freeing experience on the NAF. No judgment, just pure exploration, not knowing where one is stepping.

The expression which can be accessed in even one breath is a triumph in an unexplored musical moment. Breath by breath, the illumination of Spirit's inspired expression awaits. The flute gives voice to the sounds of our inner muse.

It can be said that the longest journey is from the head to the heart. The NAF is the perfect companion to take on that journey.

This book covers both playing from the heart as well as learning written flute music. Both are wonderful ways we can enjoy our NAF. When we play from the heart, it is complete freedom. There is no worry of playing a "wrong" note that would be obvious in a familiar tune. Instead, we access a delicate and profound space where there is no concern of playing "right" or "wrong" notes.

Hear the voice of musical freedom inviting us to let go of any need to play for performance sake. The NAF awaits our surrender to Spirit. Playing from the heart means coming from a place of openness, inquisitiveness, and vulnerability. The moment is alive and fresh.

At first, the lack of structure may feel too open. If so, the invitation is offered in that moment. Gently drop into your heart. Take a nice deep breath in, stay on the pentatonic scale, and open up. Inspiration can take you, through your flute, to a place of peace, harmony, and relaxation.

This delightful practice is the gift I wish for the flute players and soon-to-be flute players now reading this book. May the winds of heaven dance within you and your flute.

Discover yourself as an intuitive musician as you play from the heart.

Note: A blank version of this template as well as the **NAF Weekly Practice** template is found at the end of this book. Here is an example of a beginner's practice.

NAF Daily Practice

Aim for 20 - 30 minutes play time.

Start with long tones. One long breath, one long note. Go up the pentatonic scale one note at a time.
Next, take a deep breath and slowly play up the whole scale in one breath, then another to come back down.

Dexterity Practice - 5 minutes and worth every second!

Exercise	Metronome	
Long Tones with no metronome *Neighboring Notes with a metronome*	1st time	**60 bpm**
	2nd time	**63 bpm**
	3rd time	**66 bpm**

Songs I'm working on:

Song	1st time BPM	2nd time BPM	Play without the metronome
The Scale Song	*None used*		
Neighboring Notes Song	*60 bpm*	*63 bpm*	
Jumps and Neighboring Notes Improv	*None used*		

Review

Check the block when you first pick up your NAF, before you play. Align it squarely just slightly above the top edge of the sound hole. Be sure it is aligned properly and tied down snugly for good tonal quality.

Close the holes completely. Any hole that you close must be completely covered or the flute will produce a squeaky sound.

Play slowly by taking your time with every note. This will help you develop good habits. Fingering speed will come by itself.

Breathe at normal intervals for YOU. Try not to wait until you feel the need to gasp for air. Breath capacity varies from person to person. Your capacity will develop over time. Do what is comfortable for you. Breathe as often as you need.

To learn the tonal range of each note, blow softly at first, and then increase your breath.

Play LONG tones. One breath, one LONG note.

Each note has a sweet (sounding) spot. If a note is shrill or breathy, decrease the air flow. If it is wispy or weak, increase the air flow to liven it up.

Play the scale. Playing the basic scale proficiently is the foundation from which you will build your melodies. Play the scale from the bottom up and then go back down. Increase the air flow as you play up the scale and decrease it on your way back down.

As you practice LONG tones, close your eyes. This develops your tactile skills and your muscle memory, helping sensitivity develop more quickly.

Use my SoundCloud recordings to become familiar with the tones of the pentatonic scale. Go to **https://soundcloud.com/ami-sarasvati**

Practice in front of the mirror to see where there is air still leaking. This will produce a squeaking sound. Coverage must be 100% for good tonal quality.

Listen to this played on SoundCloud: **https://soundcloud.com/ami-sarasvati**

Welcome Song

by Ami Sarasvati

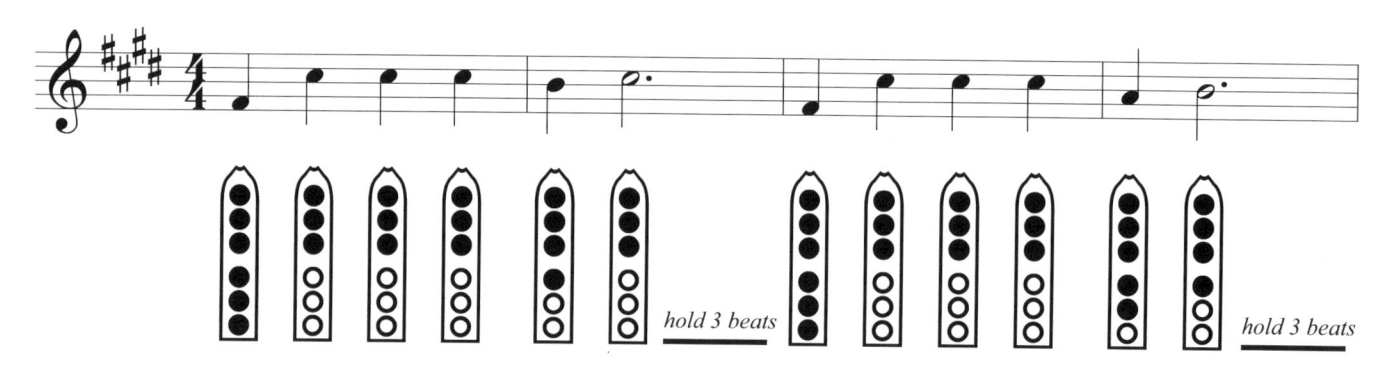

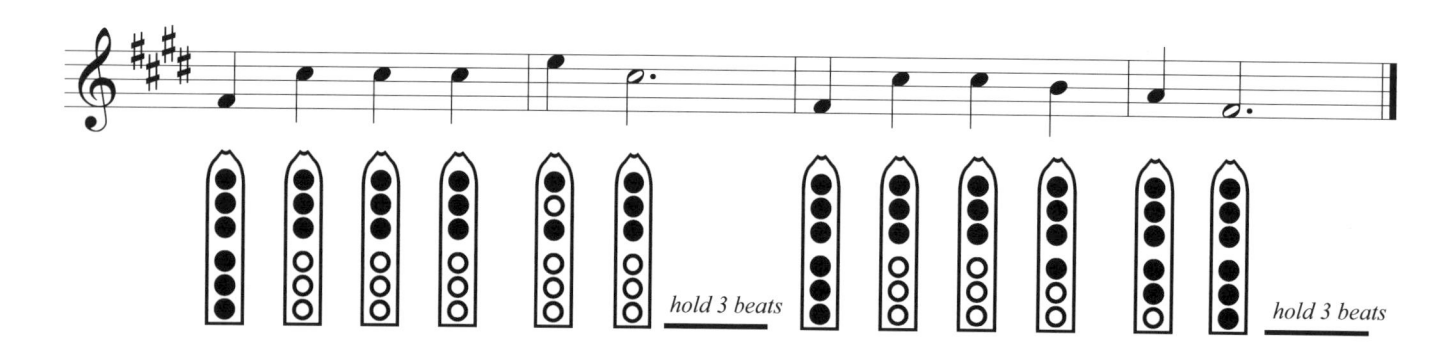

Welcome Song is great to play along to Track 3 or other tracks on *Rhythms to Accompany the Native Flute CD* by the late Stephen DeRuby.

Welcome Song is Track 2 on my CD, *One Life*, and is played with an improvisation.

Both CDs are available on Amazon.

Community Music Making

Playing music with others, when in a supportive and inclusive environment, is a great joy and an exciting musical journey. If you feel intimidated about playing with others, consider that the group mindset is more important than the individual levels of mastery on any instrument.

Have you ever seen a flock of birds suddenly change direction? The entire group finds their place quickly and unites in their flight direction. To travel harmoniously and efficiently, the community flies in the same direction, unified and without discord. It may take a few seconds, but somehow it is done naturally and gracefully. This is the concept of the Pod Mind and one that is an ideal mindset when playing music with others. It doesn't matter if it is two people playing together or a large group, the communal mind and implied commitment of all players makes for a successful group experience.

For example, in a well-run flute or drum circle, it works well when all players have been instructed in basic group music etiquette. Best practices of playing in a group means playing your instrument so you can hear the player on your right and on your left; that everyone listens to the group sound and considers how to contribute to the whole in a harmonious and balanced way.

As the player listens to the sound of the whole and entrains to the rhythm and group soundscape, the shift from single mindedness to group unity takes place. Weaving oneself into that sound mosaic of the group is organic. As individual players express new ideas, the mosaic evolves and is ever-changing.

The healing that happens in a harmonious group sound circle is palpable and consistent. Everyone contributes and expresses their sound. Simple and complex sounds open a doorway for self expression while simultaneously contributing to the greater community experience. When we play together, we take each other in. This invites all levels of talent and inspiration in the group. Truly, improvisational music is an outstanding platform to create group resonance where we meet each other in a place of inclusion and compassion.

Playing in community offers a unique way to discover your heartsong. How do you find your place in community? What kind of sound do you choose to offer? Take notice of yourself as you play with others, without judgment. Just notice how you show up in community and adjust accordingly. Do you become competitive or supportive internally? Are you okay with what you have to offer? For beginners, getting past any insecurities and self criticism can be a big hurdle. The most important point to remember is to show up for the greater good of the group and consider what you can contribute to the whole. This can be a metaphor in our daily lives for spiritual development.

Go to:
www.learntoplaynaf.com/student-area
for videos demonstrating different ideas.

Written Music Basics

This book covers a very a basic rhythm section. If you are going to play with other musicians, or you are playing familiar music to a backtrack rhythm, you will need to know a little about musical notation, timing, and other concepts to follow a rhythmic timeline. You do not need extensive music theory education, but simply a few pages of your "need to know" items for this kind of playing.

Components of Written Music

Staff: the five parallel lines upon which the notes are written.

Measure: the visual unit marked off by vertical lines that contains the counted number of beats defined by the time signature.

Measures 1   2   3   4

Time Signature: the rhythm in which the song is written.

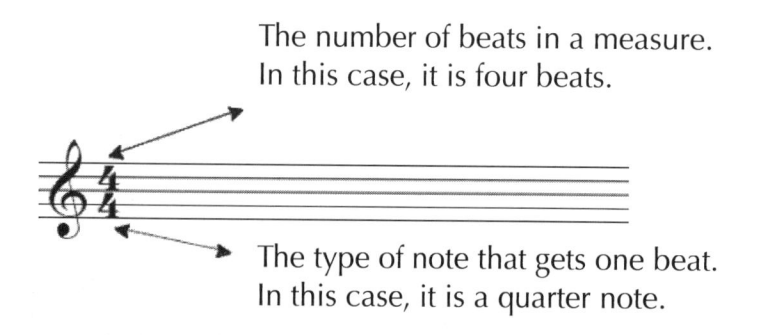

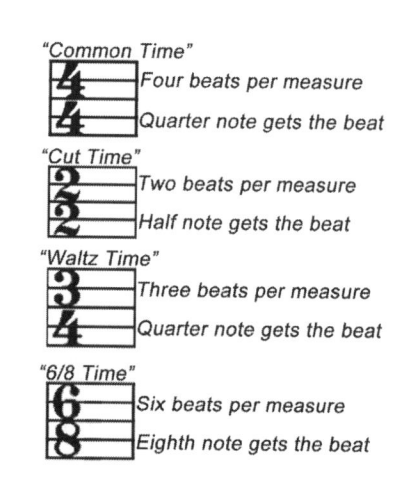

The number of beats in a measure.
In this case, it is four beats.

The type of note that gets one beat.
In this case, it is a quarter note.

"Common Time"
4/4 — Four beats per measure
Quarter note gets the beat

"Cut Time"
2/2 — Two beats per measure
Half note gets the beat

"Waltz Time"
3/4 — Three beats per measure
Quarter note gets the beat

"6/8 Time"
6/8 — Six beats per measure
Eighth note gets the beat

Basic Rhythmic Notation

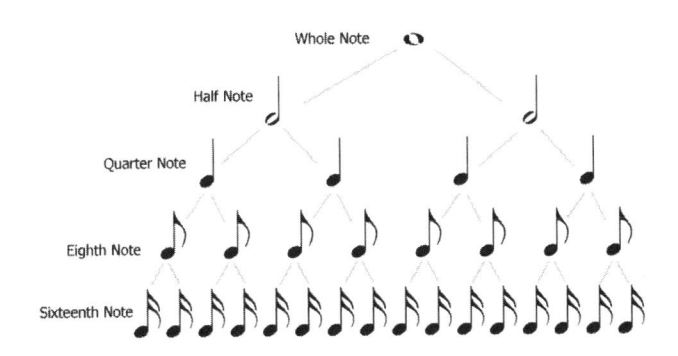

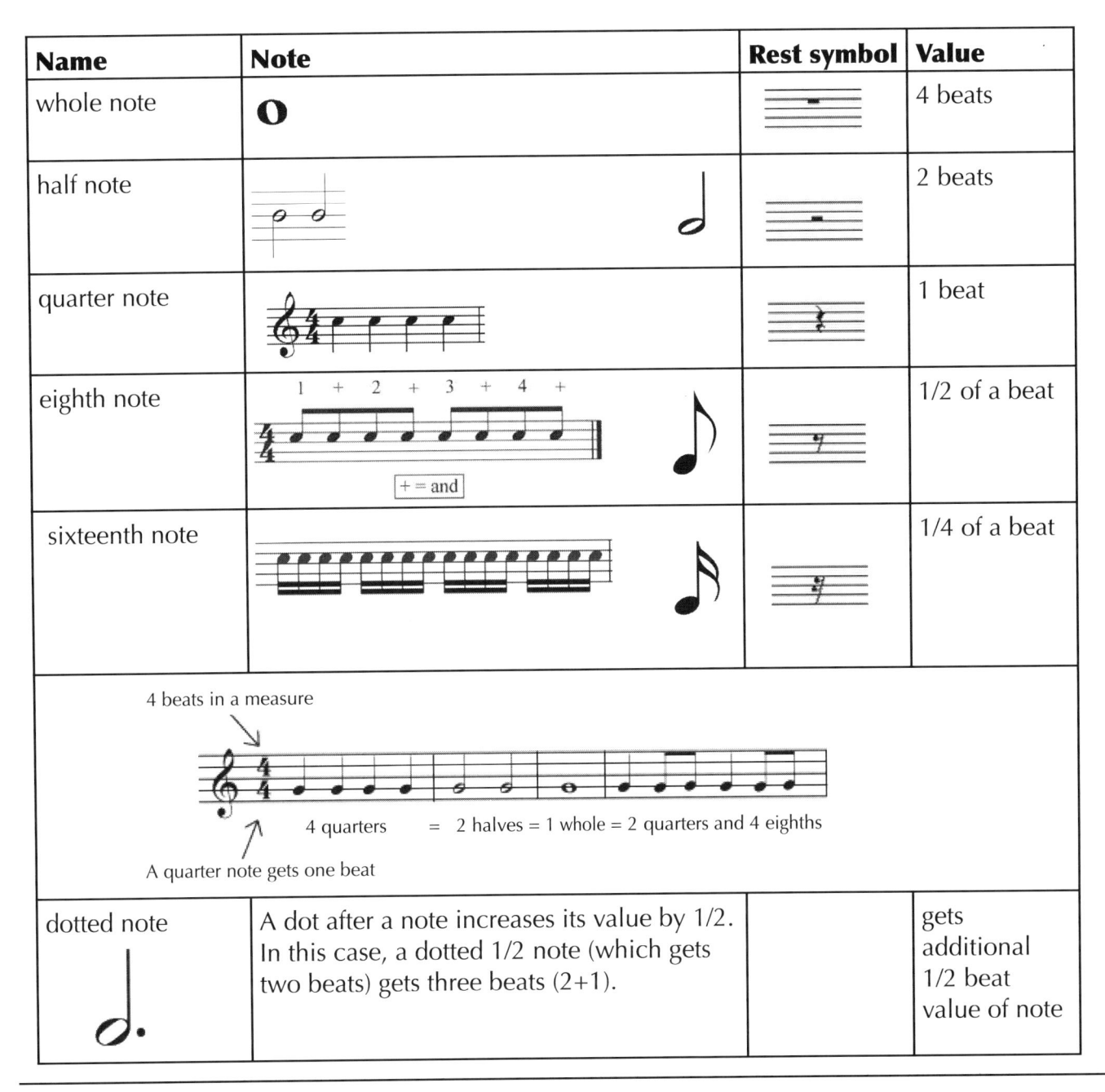

Name	Note	Rest symbol	Value
whole note	𝑜		4 beats
half note			2 beats
quarter note			1 beat
eighth note	(1 + 2 + 3 + 4 +) + = and		1/2 of a beat
sixteenth note			1/4 of a beat
	4 beats in a measure / A quarter note gets one beat / 4 quarters = 2 halves = 1 whole = 2 quarters and 4 eighths		
dotted note	A dot after a note increases its value by 1/2. In this case, a dotted 1/2 note (which gets two beats) gets three beats (2+1).		gets additional 1/2 beat value of note

Rhythm Exercises

My CD, *ONE LIFE*, Available on Amazon

I created *ONE LIFE* to support my students' progress while working through this course. It has six songs I wrote, two famous NAF songs (*Lakota Courting Song* which has a duet arrangement and an extended improvisation, and *Kiowa Love Song* with an extended improvisation), and an improvised piece with a harp player. At the end of the CD, there are four tracks in the keys of A, G, F#, and D for students to improvise over. These tracks are me playing the drone over Track 3 from Stephen DeRuby's *Rhythms to Accompany the Native Flute*.

ONE LIFE is my musical interpretation of the stages of one life.

EarthSong* - When the soul is ready to embody, it sings its song on the way to the earth plane.
Welcome Song* - At the time of birth, it sings a stable and steady song as it entrains to the earth's pulse.
Spring Dance* - The soul dances in the delight of childhood. This is a great example of playing the major scale on the NAF.
Walking in the Woods* - An alternative scale creates a different mood. Hear the wonderment of adolescence.
Lakota Courting Song - Duet arrangement. What a joy it is to play with others.
Lakota Courting Song - Improvisation example. Have some fun with it!
Kiowa Love Song - Improvisation expressing the sweet experience of being in love.
Amazing Grace - Dedicated to my Mom. She has shown grace in every way all of my life.
Gratitude* - Played on DeRuby EZ Anasazi flute in C. Surrendering to pure gratitude.
Communion* - The time comes for all of us when we rejoin Spirit and our physical body fades from this life.
The Dream - An improvisation honoring the space between lifetimes, a time to reflect, a time to review.

* indicates original songs by Ami Sarasvati

www.learntoplayNAF.com

Volume and Pitch

Discover the range of tonality of each note as you go from a low to a high volume of breath on each note. Pay close attention to what you hear and find the sweet spot of each tone.

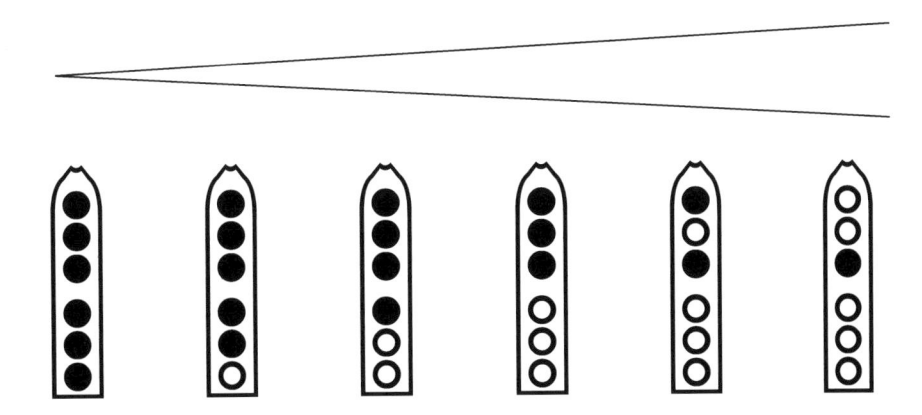

Starting on the bottom note, breathe as little as you can into your flute so you barely make a sound. Increase your breath until you're blowing as hard as you can into the flute. On the bottom note, the tone will actually break up to the octave note. Don't hold back! Explore the range of each note and notice what happens as you go up the scale.

Do you hear how, on the bottom note, very little breath is needed to make a quality sound? Yet on the top note, quite a bit of breath is required to make a quality sound. At first this may seem counterintuitive. One might initially think you need a lot of breath for the low note and just a little for the high notes. But no! Try playing the top note on your flute softly. It likely will sound more like a weak whistle than a good tone. Lots of breath is required on the top note and even more is required on the notes above the octave. When playing high notes, think *loud and proud!*

The volume of breath also differs depending on what flute you are playing. Some flutes require a very, very soft breath on the bottom note or the tone will break up to the octave (overblowing). Other flutes allow you to push it more.

You will need to get to know how each of your flutes behaves with varying volumes of breath. Take your time and get to know the nuances of each of your flutes. Trust your ear.

Adding Color, Depth, and Spice with Ornaments

Ornaments add texture, color, and artistry to your playing. Videos and live instruction are the best ways to learn these. Go to www.learntoplaynaf.com for instructional videos. Watch and listen, then experiment on your own. Describing some of these ornaments is like describing the taste of chocolate. Sometimes you just have to taste the chocolate to "understand" it! Likewise, actually hearing ornaments and seeing how they are made are the best mediums for instruction.

Here is a beginning list of the ornaments to explore on the NAF.

- slurring and tonguing
- the grace note
- the mordent
- the trill
- double and triple tonguing: say "ta-ka-ta-ka" into your flute as you play a note
- the slide and the bend
- rolling your R's (like in Spanish) while playing a note

Here are descriptions of a few ornaments:

• Tonguing
Sustain playing one note for a long breath and as you do, say "ta!" with a little burst of breath into the flute. Now try it multiple times—"ta! ta! ta!". Notice how this creates a new note, yet you are on the same pitch. Imagine playing a piano and pressing the same key down again and again.

• Chirping, then Trilling
When you are lingering on one note, for example, with all holes covered, for a quick moment, "blink" the bottom finger up for a moment and put it right back down to add texture to a long hold. This can be done on any note, although some fingers are easier than others to quickly lift and lower. Doing this multiple times creates a trill.

• Play the bottom note. While keeping all your fingers down and your seal on the flute, say "WHAT!" into the flute while adding a final burst of breath. This is a common way to finish a song.

• Vibrato
Vibrato is your all-purpose ornament and can hardly be overused. As you are playing a note, imagine a tiny birthday cake with many tiny candles on it. Blow them out one at a time as you play. Experiment with fluctuating your breath. Practice this slowly at first. Speed and proficiency will come. Before you know it, you will be adding vibrato without even thinking about it.

Listen to this played on SoundCloud: **https://soundcloud.com/ami-sarasvati**

Lakota Courting Song

Traditional

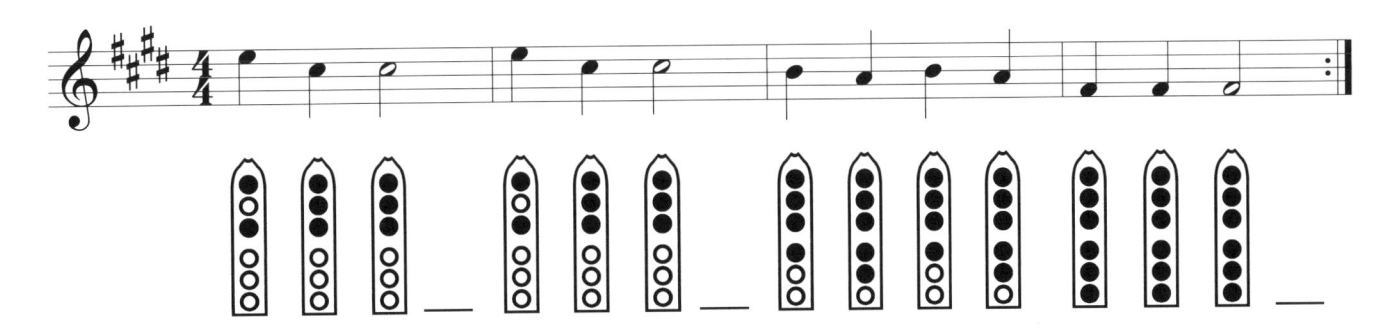

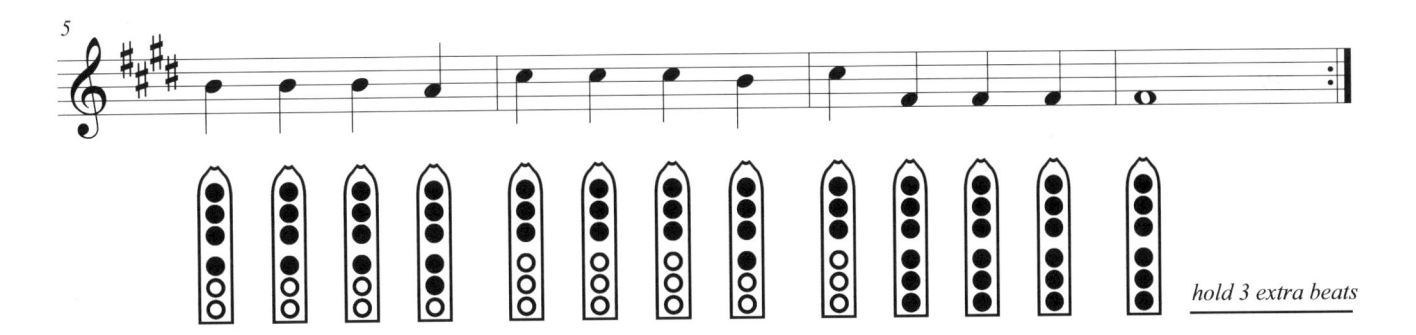

hold 3 extra beats

Lakota Courting Song is great to play along to many of the tracks on *Rhythms to Accompany the Native Flute* CD by Stephen DeRuby.

Lakota Courting Song as a duet arrangement is found later in this book. On my CD, *One Life*, tracks #5 and #6 offer two variations of this beloved song—one as a duet and one as an extended improvisation.

This page is intended to inspire you to take the next step with your NAF playing. With a simple song like this, the flute diagrams are easy enough to read, but there is a system that is easy to learn and widely used in NAF music, which is **Nakai Tab.** Although lots of music is available for the Native American style flute using the flute diagrams, it is the author's recommendation that students take the time to learn Nakai Tab which looks like standard musical notation. Understanding the rhythm clearly using Nakai Tab is reason enough to learn it. There are only 15 notes to master in the system. You can do it!

The next section of the book will provide you the tools you need to learn Nakai Tab. I've gone through this process for years with students online, and as long as they really dug in on the next few pages, they were able to get comfortable with this wonderful system. First, a bit about R. Carlos Nakai.

About R. Carlos Nakai

R. Carlos Nakai is a Native American of Navajo and Ute heritage. He is the most widely known Native American flute player in the world and is largely credited with the renaissance of this wonderful instrument. The proper pronunciation of "Nakai" rhymes with "hawkeye." As a college student, he played brass instruments. He was in an auto accident which damaged his mouth, making it impossible to produce the correct embouchure to continue playing brass instruments. He was given a traditional Native American cedar flute and challenged to master it.

Nakai developed a system of tablature notation (commonly known as Nakai Tablature or Nakai TAB) that can be used across the spectrum of Native American style flute keys. He published this in *The Art of the Native American Flute* (1996) with James Demars, Ken Light, and David P. McAllester. He has produced numerous CDs and performs regularly.

Discover R. Carlos Nakai on the internet to understand the depth of his work with the Native American flute. Nakai's website is: www.rcarlosnakai.com.

Here's the "fine print" about the key signature of four sharps for the NAF:

From www.flutopedia.com/nakai_tablature.htm:
"Recall that most Native American flutes are tuned to a minor key, so we need to find the 'key of F# minor'. But now, realize that there are quite a few different flavors of 'minor keys', each with their own key signature. The most commonly used minor key in the Western classical music (and, by extension, most popular music), is called the 'Natural Minor' (also called the Aeolean mode). However, the 'key of F# natural minor' has the notes: F#, G#, A, B, C#, D, E. Note that there are three sharps, and so the key of F# natural minor has three sharps. However, based on discussions with R. Carlos Nakai and Ron Warren, it has been observed that the most common tunings of traditional Native American flutes have the notes: F#, G#, A, B, C#, D#, E ... four sharps. Rather than Aeolean mode, this is a different mode called Dorian mode (also called 'Russian minor', and is used by popular songs such as Scarborough Fair). So, Nakai Tablature uses the 'key of F# Dorian mode', or four sharps."

All above three photos: Photography: by John Running. Courtesy of Canyon Records.

What Nakai himself writes about Nakai Tablature

From Nakai's *The Art of the Native American Flute* ([Nakai 1996]:
"In an effort to simplify the transition from one flute to another (e.g. changing from a flute in F-sharp minor to G minor), I have maintained the same notation for all flutes. These instruments produce the same series of musical intervals as the F-sharp minor flute but the pitches are transposed so that the scale begins on the same fundamental tone. The lower tone is played with all finger holes closed and is written as F-sharp (F#) but the actual sounded pitch will vary from one flute to another. The correlation of actual pitch to finger notation is easily and readily determined by cross-referencing the line for the key of your Native American flute and the column in which the tablature notation occurs. Each Native American flute uses the very same fingerings, from all-closed to middle three, and by using a digital tuner or well-tuned piano the actual pitches can be written in their exact notational positions over the tablature notation."

Photo taken at the Musical Instrument Museum in Phoenix, AZ in 2012.

To begin learning Nakai Tab, let's start with:

The Pentatonic Scale of the Native American Style Flute

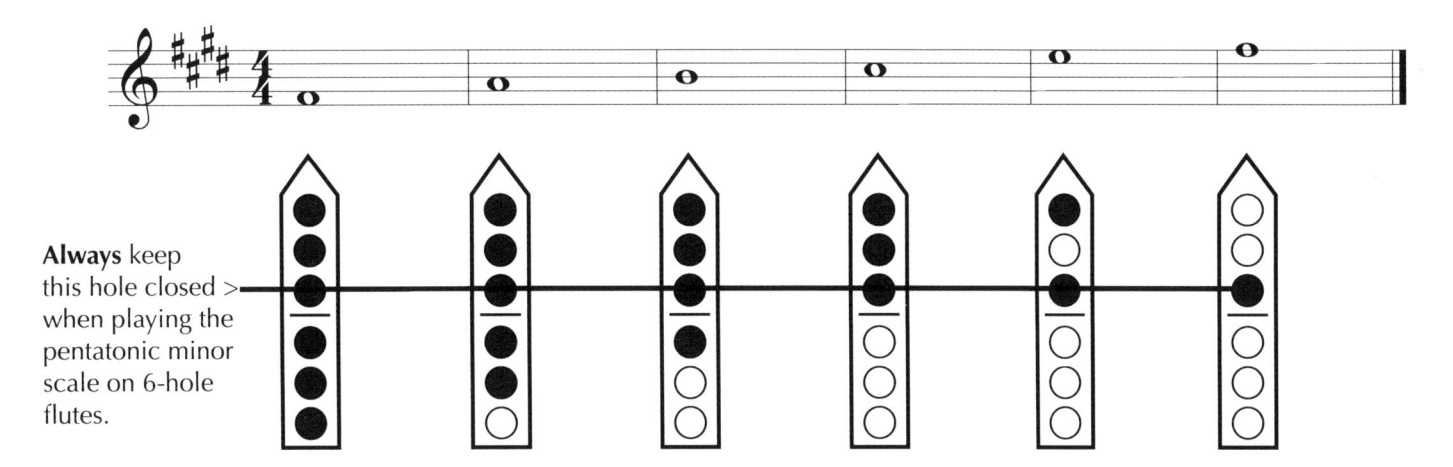

Always keep this hole closed > when playing the pentatonic minor scale on 6-hole flutes.

Clarifying point for musicians who already know how to read music: the notes used in Nakai Tab are *technically* F#, A, B, C#, E, and F# (octave note) according to the four sharps in the key signature Nakai Tab is based upon.

For the purpose of learning the pentatonic scale and using the Nakai Tab system, these notes are simply referred to with their note name. We do not say F sharp or C sharp, we simply say F and C.

From the bottom up, we play one note at a time (keeping the fourth hole from the bottom on 6-hole flutes closed) and we call the notes F, A, B, C, E, F (which is one octave above the root note). As noted above, if you are playing a 6-hole flute, **the ring finger of the top hand is always kept down.**

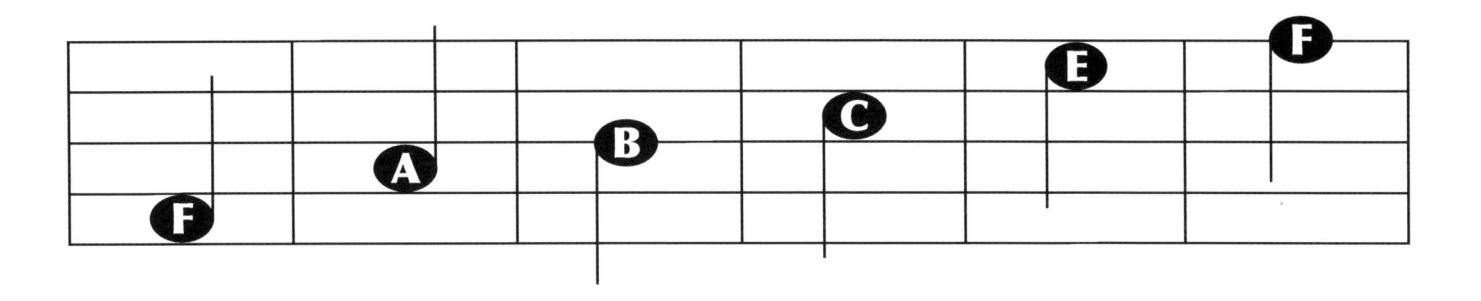

Bottom Hand Notes

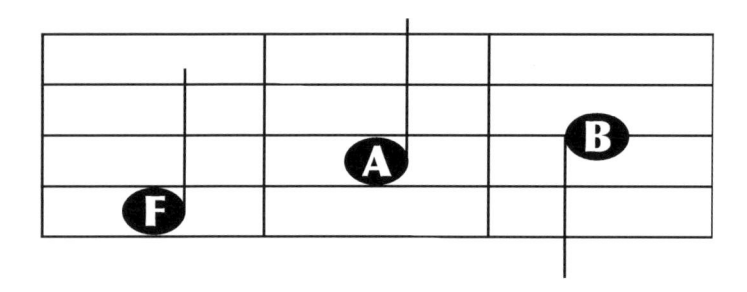

Notice where each note is placed on the staff. Is it on a space or a line? Which space? Which line?

Bottom Hand Practice
Go slowly. Aim for accuracy and evenness. See directions on top of next page.

Rewrite the bottom hand practice lines, one at a time, paying close attention to where the note lands on the staff. Start by marking off four measures.

Write a 2-line song using bottom hand notes with four measures on each line.

Top Hand Notes

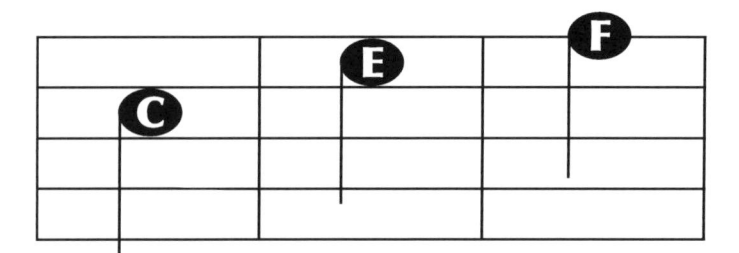

Notice where each note is placed on the staff. Is it on a space or a line? Which space? Which line?

Top Hand Practice
Go slowly. Aim for accuracy and evenness. See directions on top of next page.

Rewrite the top hand practice lines, one at a time, paying close attention to where the note lands on the staff. Start by marking off four measures.

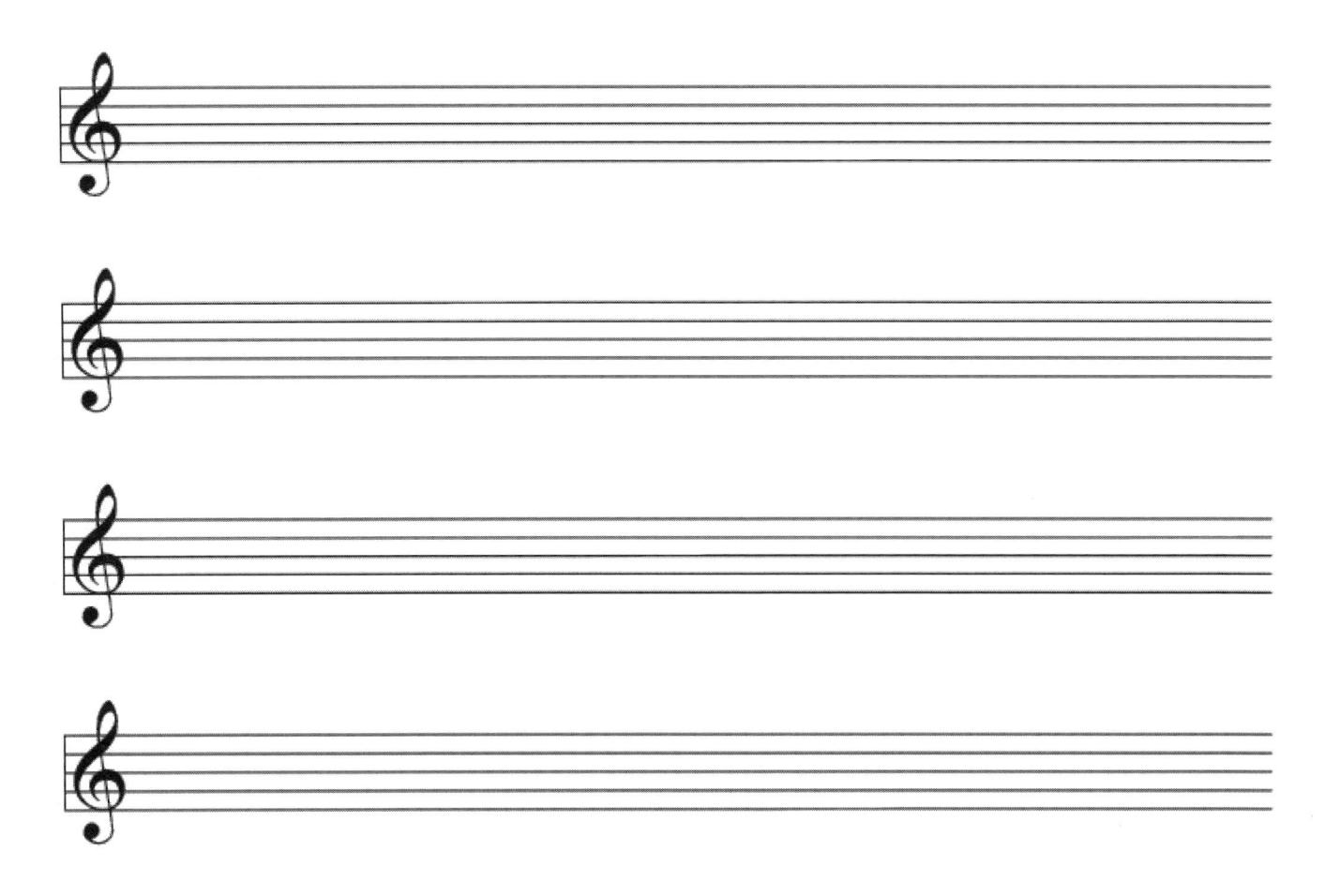

Write a 2-line song using top hand notes with four measures on each line.

Putting it all together

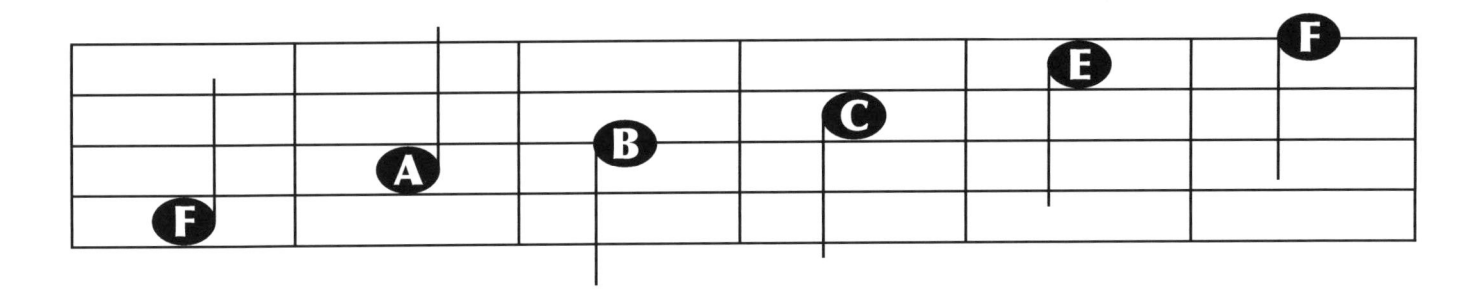

See directions on top of next page.

Welcome Song

by Ami Sarasvati

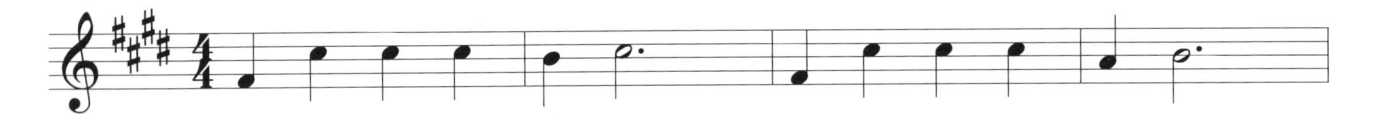

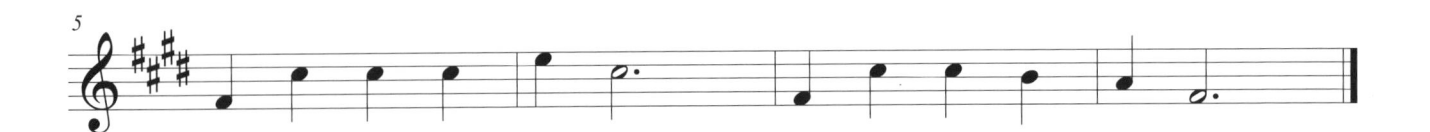

Rewrite the Welcome Song using Nakai Tab.

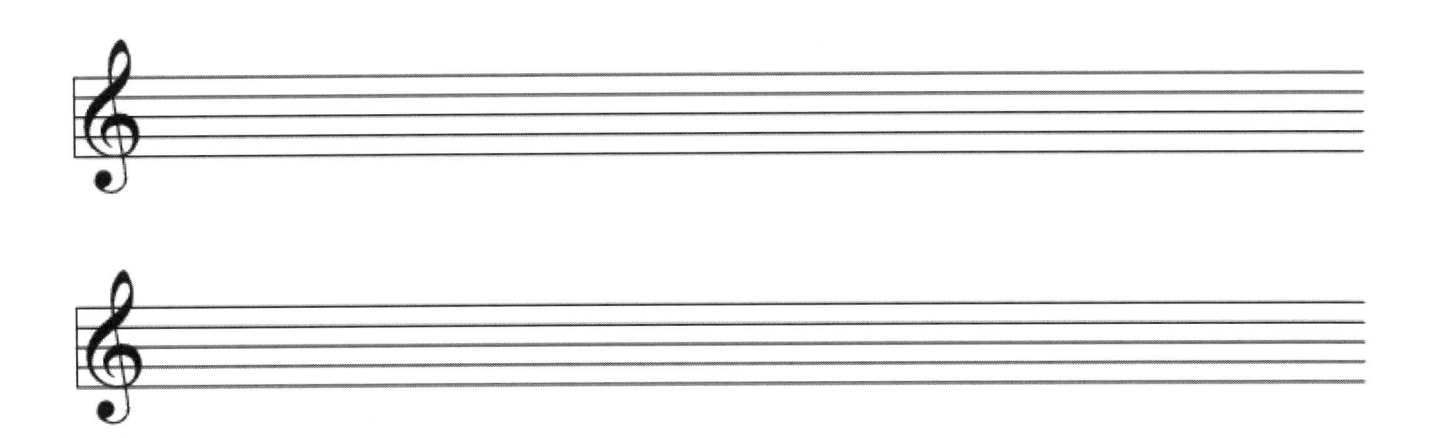

Write a two line song in Nakai Tab using all the notes of the pentatonic scale. End your song on the bottom note.

Nakai TAB Practice

More Nakai TAB Practice

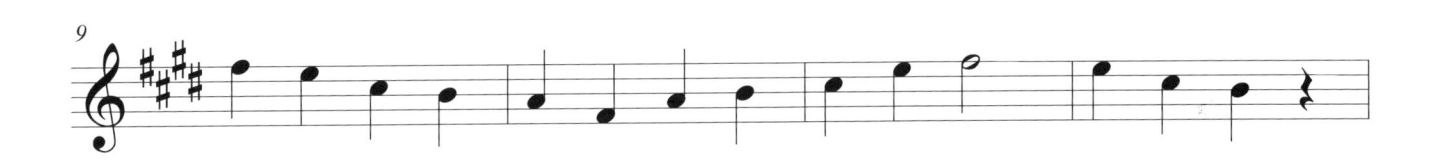

Lakota Courting Song
(Duet Arrangement)

Traditional
Duet arrangement by Ami Sarasvati

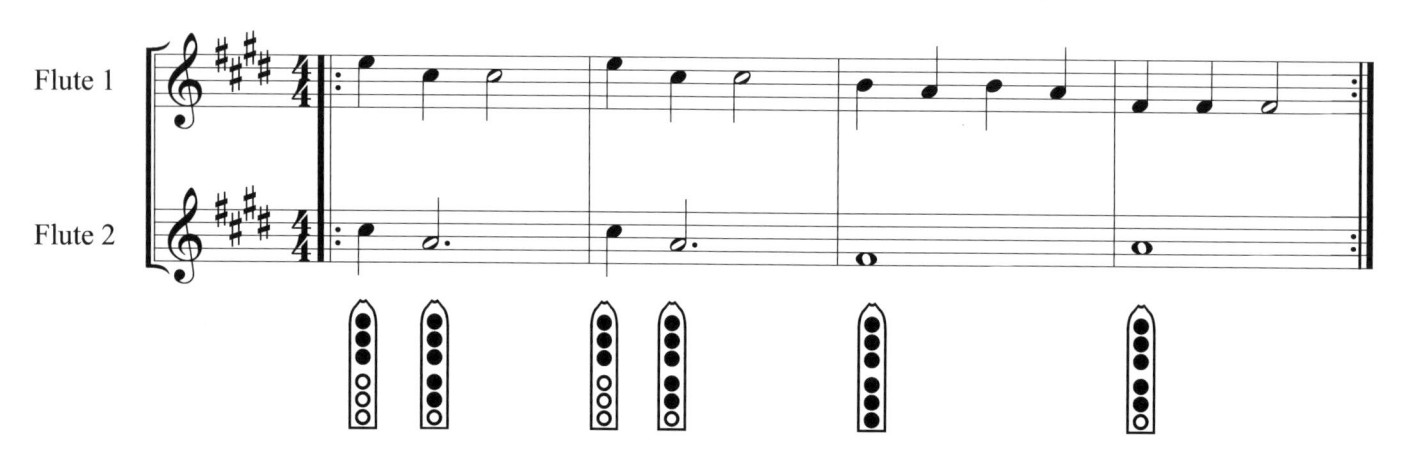

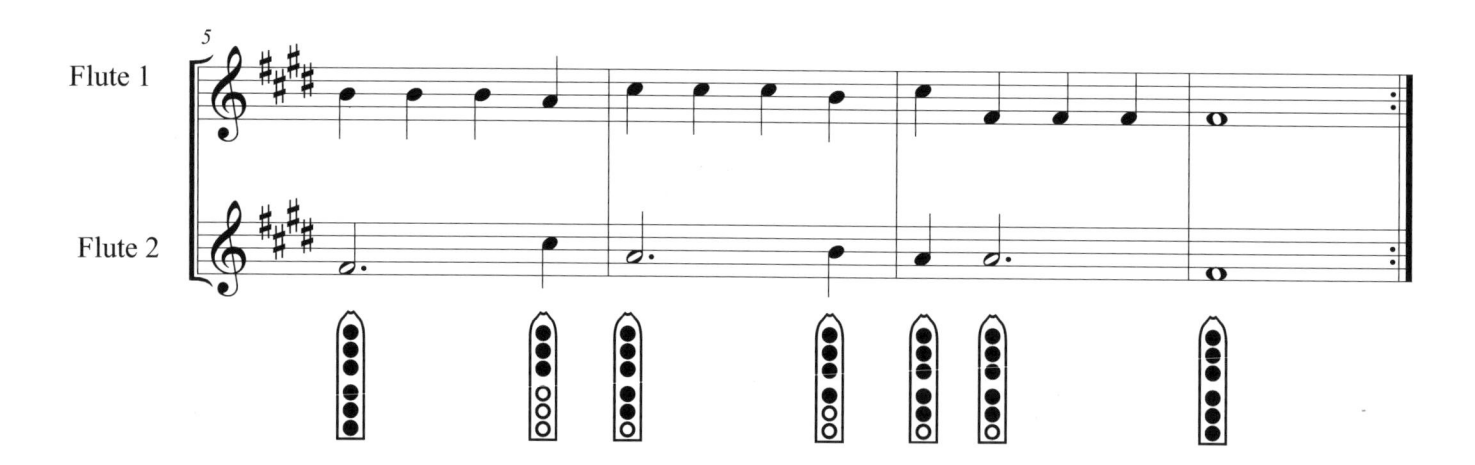

Note: *The Lakota Courting Song,* illustrating Nakai tab and flute diagrams for Flute 1, is found earlier in this book. On this duet arrangement, I have included both Nakai tab and flute diagrams for Flute 2.

Pranayama

In Sanskrit, an ancient language of India dating back over 3,500 years, the practice of regulating the breath is called pranayama. In nearly all Yoga styles, pranayama is the central focus of the practice. Breathwork is thousands of years old for a reason. Specific breathing techniques yield a myriad of benefits to the body, mind, emotions, and spirit. Regular practice results in more energy, increased awareness, and improved cardiovascular function.

What does pranayama have to do with discovering your heartsong on the NAF? Playing flute is a musical form of pranayama. When we consciously bring Spirit in through the breath and surrender to the moment, the flute becomes the co-creator of our heartsong. In the words of Yogi Bhajan, the Master of Kundalini Yoga, "Your breath is the voice of your soul."

As a spiritual practice, breathwork gives us immediate access to inner wisdom which has an intelligence all its own. As a simple practice, we can drop into our heart space as we inhale. Feel the heart's rhythm. Like waves in the ocean, the breath comes through the body again and again to inspire our playing. Each wave is another glimpse into the mystery.

As our skill level increases and we can confidently maneuver on the NAF, Spirit rejoices amid the intervals and the breath. The breath gives the emotions a metaphoric hand to hold and a vehicle for release.

Playing the flute is a healing art. Within the practice, a great deal of breath is required. Even playing a few minutes yields a more fully oxygenated state. The player receives profound benefits simply from the required deep breathing. Each sacred breath informs the frequencies released by the flute. These vibrations voiced through the flute, played skillfully and from the heart, have the power to heal the player as well as all who listen.

Trapped emotions in the body can be detrimental to our health. Breathwork can assist us in accessing, processing, and transmuting these emotions. A very simple daily practice with the NAF gives us a way to express our innermost emotions in a peaceful and natural way.

Note:
Flute players may experience a light trance state from the deep breathing combined with the haunting tones coming from the flute.

If you feel lightheaded, be assured your body is adjusting to the marked increase in oxygen. Take a short break, perhaps get a glass of water, and just relax until it passes. As the body adjusts to your new muse, pranayama extends a delightful benefit to your practice.

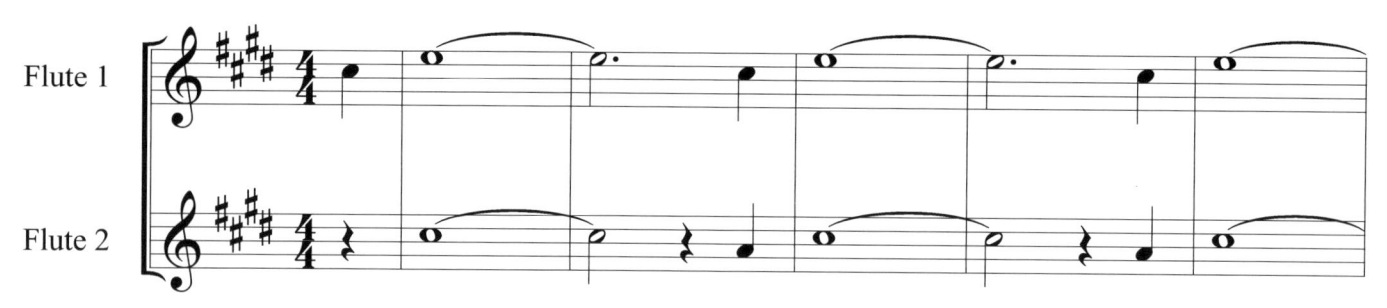

Zuni Sunrise
(Duet Arrangement)

Traditional
Duet arrangement by Ami Sarasvati

Zuni Sunrise (cont.)

Play Your NAF When You're Out and About

Playing your flute when you're out and about, especially in the good weather, is a fun way to be adventurous and start really playing from the heart. Always keep your personal safety in mind. As much as tunnels and parking garages can offer excellent acoustics, it is important to remember the realities of life and keep yourself safe. The sound of your flute will travel far and you will likely receive many wonderful comments about the playing, even when you think you're not playing well yet. Let go and let the flute play you!

A group of flute friends and I occasionally go play in a pedestrian tunnel that connects two walkways near a local college. Occasionally, cyclists, people walking their dogs, and college students pass through the tunnel. It is not a remote spot, so we feel safe. The acoustics of the tunnel make it sound like we're in the Grand Canyon. See if you can find a safe place to have this wonderful experience!

Here's a typical scene: one of us starts playing the drone. Someone else starts to solo over the drone. Then they settle into the drone and someone else goes. It goes around and around without a plan, often without words, just using visual cues and body language to communicate.

We continue this for awhile, without prior discussion or plan. It is all organic and perfect in its inception. Then someone starts with a new idea, a pattern, and the group shifts to playing with that. Then something else emerges and we all just float in this symphony we've created in this little underpass tunnel.

A musical conversation grows organically and then after a while, the flute music becomes more and more simple until it turns to just a couple notes played by one, then the other. The conversation evolves to a long tone, then a responding long tone, then somehow, players resolve on the bottom note and simultaneously create a lovely and resonant vibrato. The tones continue to float in the air and hearts of the players. It could be a thousand years ago or it could be today. The playing stops and the echoes of the flutes are in the air and in our hearts. The silence of the flutes is like a prayer released.

Any of the musical ideas on the next page can be used when gathering with one or many other flute players. Please take the time to watch the videos on www.learntoplaynaf.com/student-area to get ideas on how to play with others. It is an absolutely magical experience!

Favorite Places to Play Your NAF:
- A canyon
- In a church
- At a lake
- In a cave
- In a tunnel or passageway
- In the woods
- In the garage

Ideas for Playing with Other NAF Players

Call and Response

Call and Response can be done in a wide variety of ways. If you have two flute players, they can go back and forth with these ideas. They can be used in a circle as well.

- an alternating one breath solo
- in a fashion where each player takes their turn and plays for a little while, say for 20-30 seconds
- players establish on a basic rhythm (like short-LONG) and go back and forth, or around the circle
- players make up a little melody and they go back and forth with the musical idea
- any other ideas and inspirations that come to mind

The idea is to let your flute be your voice and have fun in the moment. It is good to keep in mind that regardless of the players' musical abilities, the time should be somewhat even. Each player is encouraged to take their turn and enjoy the opportunity to express themselves musically.

Solo over Drone

The *drone* is when someone simply plays and sustains the bottom note. Over the drone, another person plays a solo. Here are two ways to do this with multiple players.

- One way is to have a person play a solo and all the others play the drone, quietly. Then the next player gets a chance to solo while the others play the drone. Keep moving around the circle.
- Or, have one person solo and the person next to the soloist, drone. Switch to the next pair of players.

If multiple people are playing the drone while one person solos, it is best to remember to keep the drones quite soft so that the soloist can be heard. Staying on the pentatonic scale during one's solo will ensure a harmonic experience for the group.

Duets

The *Lakota Courting Song* Duet Arrangement in this book is a great song to work with in learning to play a duet with others. The one important aspect of playing to a certain timeline of rhythm is committing to staying right with the rhythm. Enjoy!

Trios

The first person plays the drone (bottom note). The second person plays an ostinato (a simple repeating pattern). The third person does a solo improvisation. After a while, rotate the parts clockwise.

Rounds

See the video "How Lovely Round" in the Student Area of my website for this example.

See the next page for videos demonstrating these ideas.

These videos demonstrate different ways to play NAF with others.

You can access these videos by going to **www.learntoplayNAF.com/student-area** or by typing these URLs into your internet search engine directly.

One breath solo, starting on and landing on any note on the pentatonic scale.
https://youtu.be/Dw5j1_m2SgE

One breath solo, starting on the note the last flute player ended on.
https://youtu.be/d0vOjuca1yA

Players having a musical conversation, one after another.
https://youtu.be/enirwFVLMt4

Solo over drone on EZ Anasazi Native Flute.
https://youtu.be/tM-DNx4tSbc

Lakota Courting Song as a duet arrangement.
https://youtu.be/O0w-VSBvWqE

Lakota Courting Song as a duet arrangement with an improvisation over drone.
https://youtu.be/MY9Jeb8MDx0

Amazing Grace as a duet arrangement.
https://youtu.be/mOts5VFWSdA

A three part round, How Lovely is the Evening.
https://youtu.be/PFoqGCbDfvI

Solo over drone, taking turns.
https://youtu.be/AYjPVp-WKSM

Another example of solo over drone, taking turns.
https://youtu.be/odkc5Dc_z_c

Yet another example of solo over drone, taking turns.
https://youtu.be/IZ90bQg4gWQ

Flute players and hand drummers play the Lakota Courting Song.
https://youtu.be/0x0Dha4GCoY

Flute players and hand drummers improvise!
https://youtu.be/InwYR8k85fI

The Major and Minor Scales

The NAF is a versatile instrument. After getting good at playing the pentatonic minor scale, you can begin to learn other scales also available. These include Middle Eastern scales, the Akebono scale, Blues scales, the Ionian mode, major scales, Mode 4, and others. For a comprehensive catalog of scales, go to **http://flutopedia.com/scales.htm**

The Minor Pentatonic Scale
This scale is the primary scale of the contemporary NAF and the one you've been working with to this point in the book. Take a few minutes and just play the scale song. Take your time on each note. Linger where you'd like to. What do you feel when you simply play the scale? Do you hear the soulfulness of this scale? When your heart is longing, grieving, or yearning for someone you love, the minor pentatonic scale can give you an outlet to express these feelings.

The Major Scale
In contrast, try using the concept of the scale song, but use only the Major scale notes (the bottom hole stays open). What do you hear? Do you sense the brightness of this scale?

The intervals on this scale are what we are used to in our Do-Re-Mi major scale.

The Major Scale

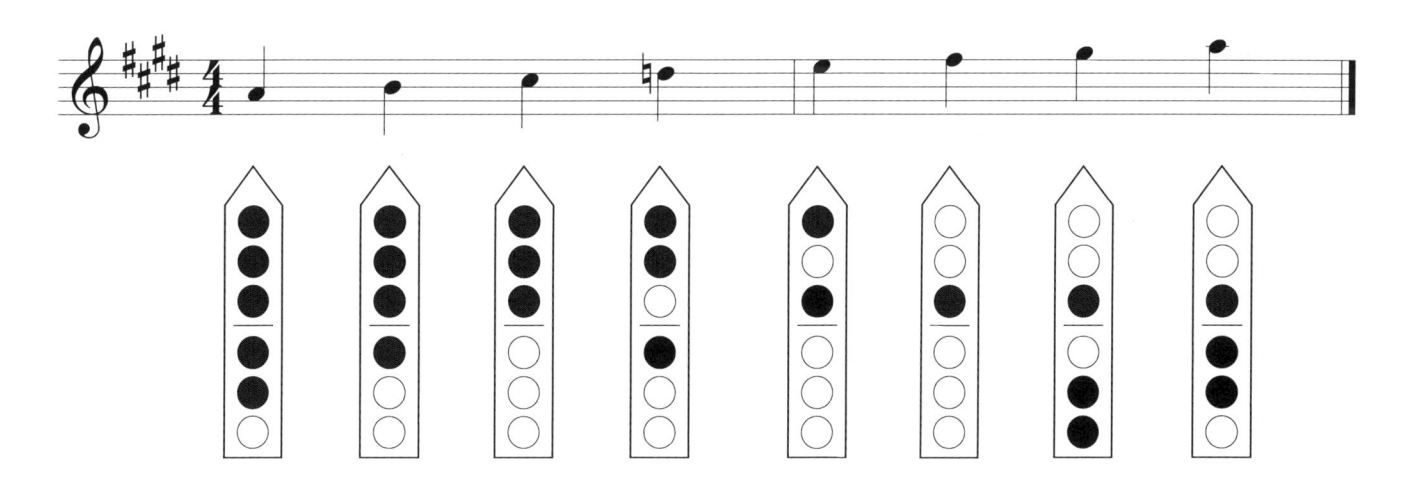

Extended Scale Notes on the NAF

The ability to play a good quality tone of the higher notes varies quite a bit from flute to flute. Not all flutes will play the higher notes well or at all. When playing the high notes, be sure to use a very strong breath.

✱ The pentatonic scale is made up of the notes with the asterisks above the flute.

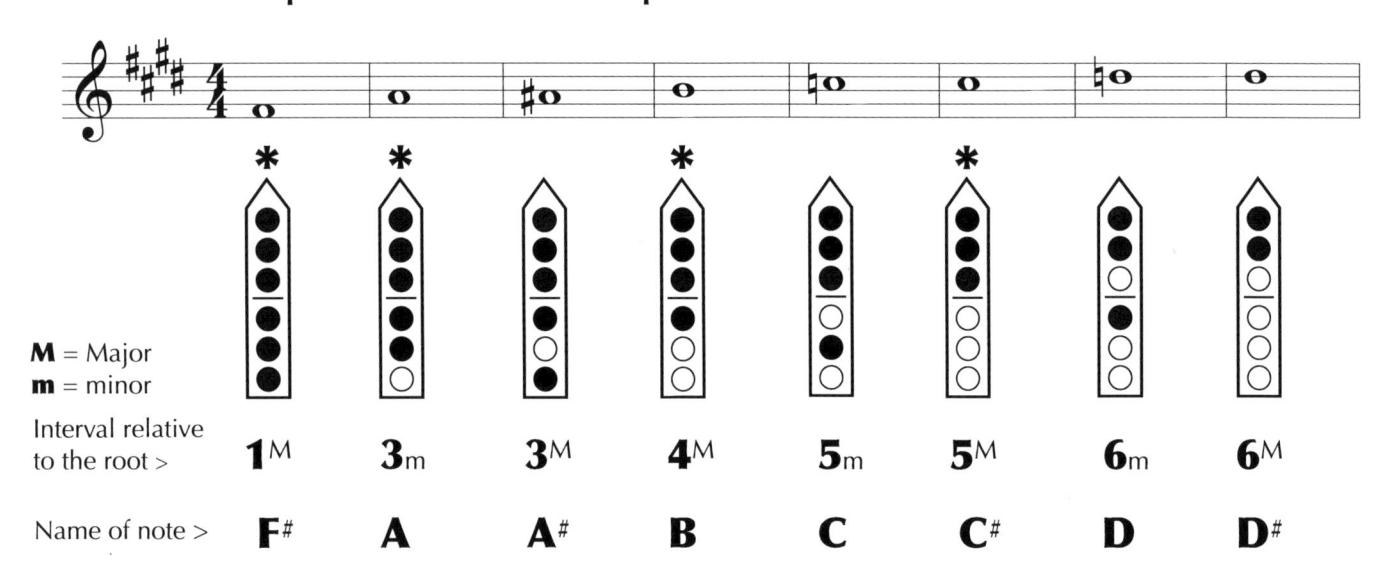

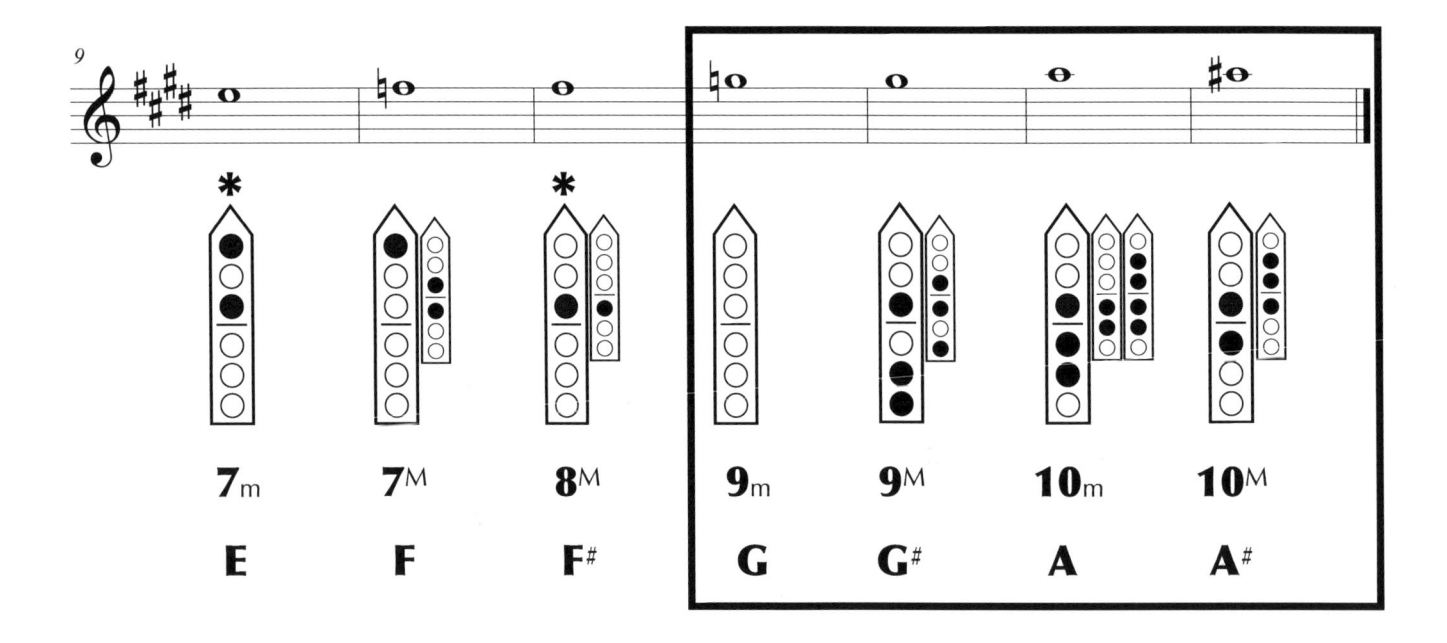

M = Major
m = minor
Interval relative to the root > 1M 3m 3M 4M 5m 5M 6m 6M

Name of note > F# A A# B C C# D D#

7m 7M 8M 9m 9M 10m 10M

E F F# G G# A A#

The smaller flutes (next to larger flutes) offer alternative finger placement of the note. On some flutes, the larger flute finger placement will work, on other flutes, the smaller flute suggestion may be better.

Mode 1 and Mode 2. These are the two primary scales of your flute. If we begin our scale with all holes covered, we are playing in Mode 1 which is a minor scale. When we start our scale on the second hole up, we are playing in Mode 2 which is a major scale and requires some cross-fingering. See the next page for more of an explanation.

Mode 1
The pentatonic minor scale starts with all holes closed.

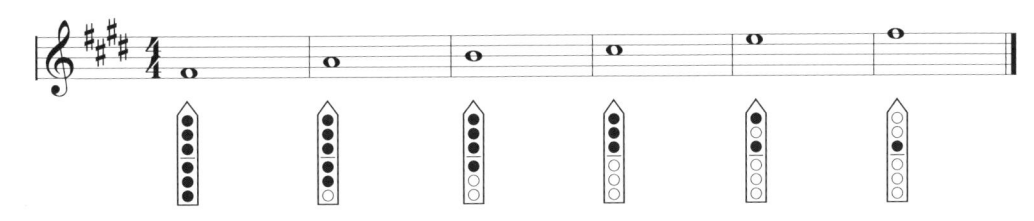

Mode 2
The major diatonic scale starts on the 2nd hole up.

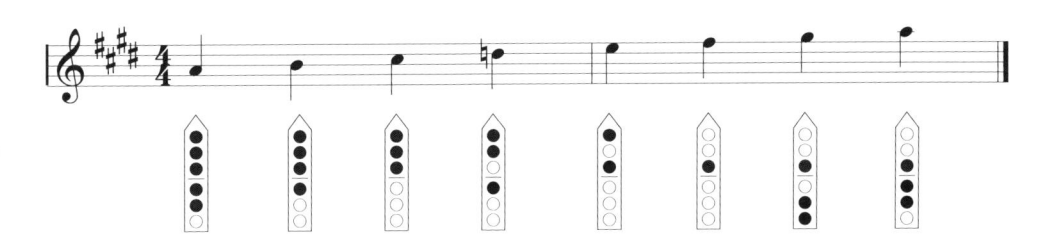

Chart of the actual note pitches on the Native American flute (o) = OCTAVE								
A minor NAF flute:								
Mode 1 (A minor)	A	C	D	E	G	A (o)		
Mode 2 (C major)	C	D	E	F	G	A	B	C (o)
C minor NAF flute:								
Mode 1 (C minor)	C	Eb	F	G	Bb	C (o)		
Mode 2 (Eb major)	Eb	F	G	Ab	Bb	C	D	Eb (o)
D minor NAF flute:								
Mode 1 (D minor)	D	F	G	A	C	D (o)		
Mode 2 (F major)	F	G	A	Bb	C	D	E	F (o)
E minor NAF flute:								
Mode 1 (E minor)	E	G	A	B	D	E (o)		
Mode 2 (G major)	G	A	B	C	D	E	F#	G (o)
F# minor NAF flute:								
Mode 1 (F# minor)	F#	A	B	C#	E	F# (o)		
Mode 2 (A major)	A	B	C#	D	E	F#	G#	A (o)
G minor NAF flute:								
Mode 1 (G minor)	G	Bb	C	D	F	G (o)		
Mode 2 (Bb major)	Bb	C	D	Eb	F	G	A	Bb (o)

www.learntoplayNAF.com

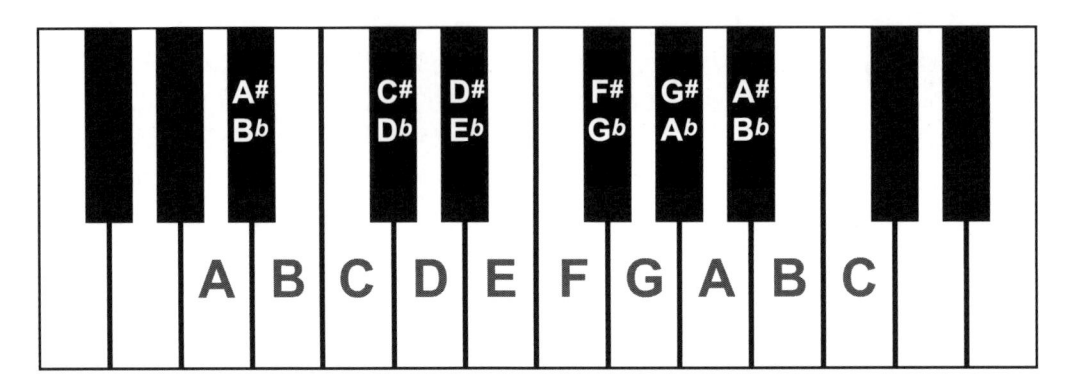

Use the keyboard to find the relative major key of your flute. Start from the bottom note and go up three half-steps (using both the white and black keys) to arrive at the beginning pitch of the major key for that flute. In other words, on an E minor flute, and looking at the keyboard, go up three half steps and you will arrive at the major key of that flute, which is G. So, your E minor flute can also play the G major scale. Starting on the second hole up from the bottom of the flute is called **Mode 2**.

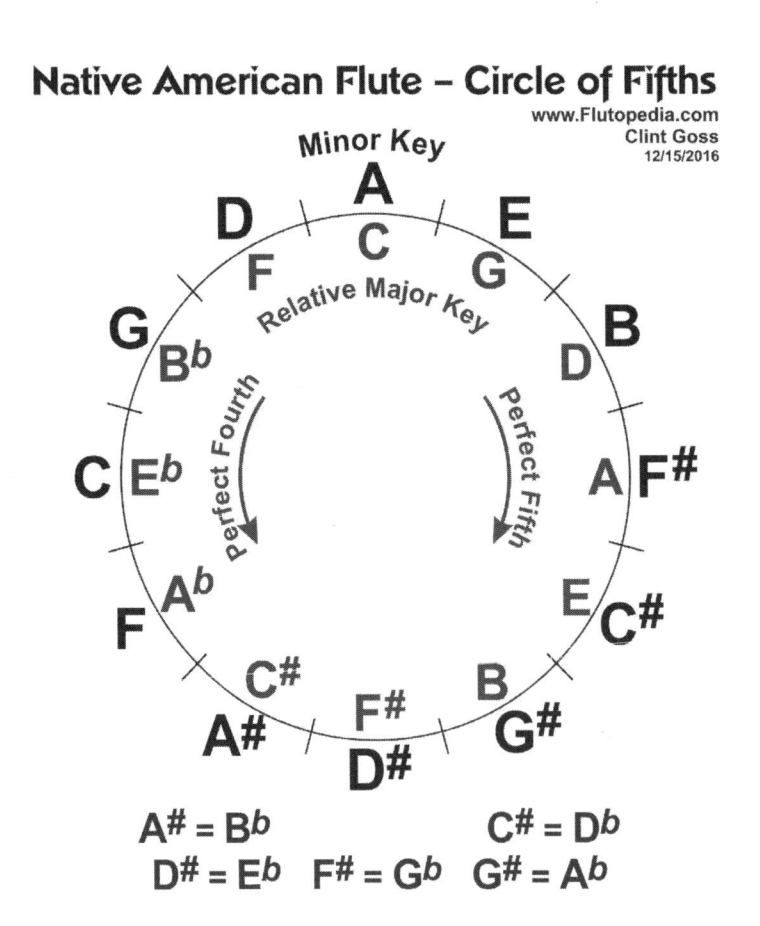

Native American Flute – Circle of Fifths

www.Flutopedia.com
Clint Goss
12/15/2016

A# = Bb   C# = Db
D# = Eb   F# = Gb   G# = Ab

Use this diagram to quickly identify the relative major key for your flutes.
Printed with permission from Clint Goss.

Go to **www.flutopedia.com** for more information.

This chart shows what guitar chords go well with Mode 1 and Mode 2 on all keys of NAFs.

	NAF Mode 1	NAF Mode 2 (Major key)	Capo on Guitar
FLUTE KEY:	E minor	G major	No capo
Guitar no capo	Em Am Bm7	G C D7	
Capo on fret 1	E^{b}m A^{b}m B^{b}m7	F# B C#7	
Capo on fret 2	Dm Gm Am7	F B^b C7	
Capo on fret 3	C#m F#m A^{b}m7	E A B7	
FLUTE KEY:	F minor	G# or A^b major	Capo 1
FLUTE KEY:	F# or G^b minor	A major	Capo 2
Guitar no capo	F#m Bm C#m7	A D E7	
Capo on fret 1	F#m B^{b}m Cm7	A^b C# E^{b}7	
Capo on fret 2	Em Am Bm7	G C D7	
Capo on fret 3	E^{b}m A^{b}m B^{b}m7	F# B C#7	
FLUTE KEY:	G minor	A# or B^b major	Capo 3
Guitar no capo	Gm Cm Dm7	B^b E^b F7	
Capo on fret 1	F#m Bm C#m7	A D E7	
Capo on fret 2	Fm B^{b}m Cm7	Ab C# E^{b}7	
Capo on fret 3	Em Am Bm7	G C D7	
FLUTE KEY:	G# or A^b minor	B major	Capo 4
FLUTE KEY:	A minor	C major	Capo 5
Guitar no capo	Am Dm Em7	C F G7	
Capo on fret 1	A^{b}m C#m E^{b}m7	B E F#7	
Capo on fret 2	Gm Cm Dm7	B^b E^b F7	
Capo on fret 3	F#m Bm C#m7	A D E7	
FLUTE KEY:	A# or B^b minor	C# or D^b major	Capo 6
FLUTE KEY:	B minor	D major	Capo 7
FLUTE KEY:	C minor	D# or E^b major	Capo 8
FLUTE KEY:	C# or D^b minor	E major	Capo 9
FLUTE KEY:	D minor	F major	Capo 10
FLUTE KEY:	D# or E^b minor	F# major	Capo 11

Spring Dance

by Ami Sarasvati

Spring Dance is a catchy tune and will help you to get really comfortable with Mode 2.

Check out the recording on:

www.soundcloud.com/ami-sarasvati

Do you hear the brightness of the major scale?
Try learning this song by listening to it a few times
on SoundCloud and then playing it by ear.

Listen to the improvisation
and come up with one on your own.

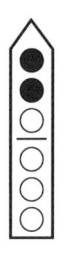

A new note—the major 6th.

6^M

D#

Amazing Grace

Traditional Folk
Arr. Ami Sarasvati

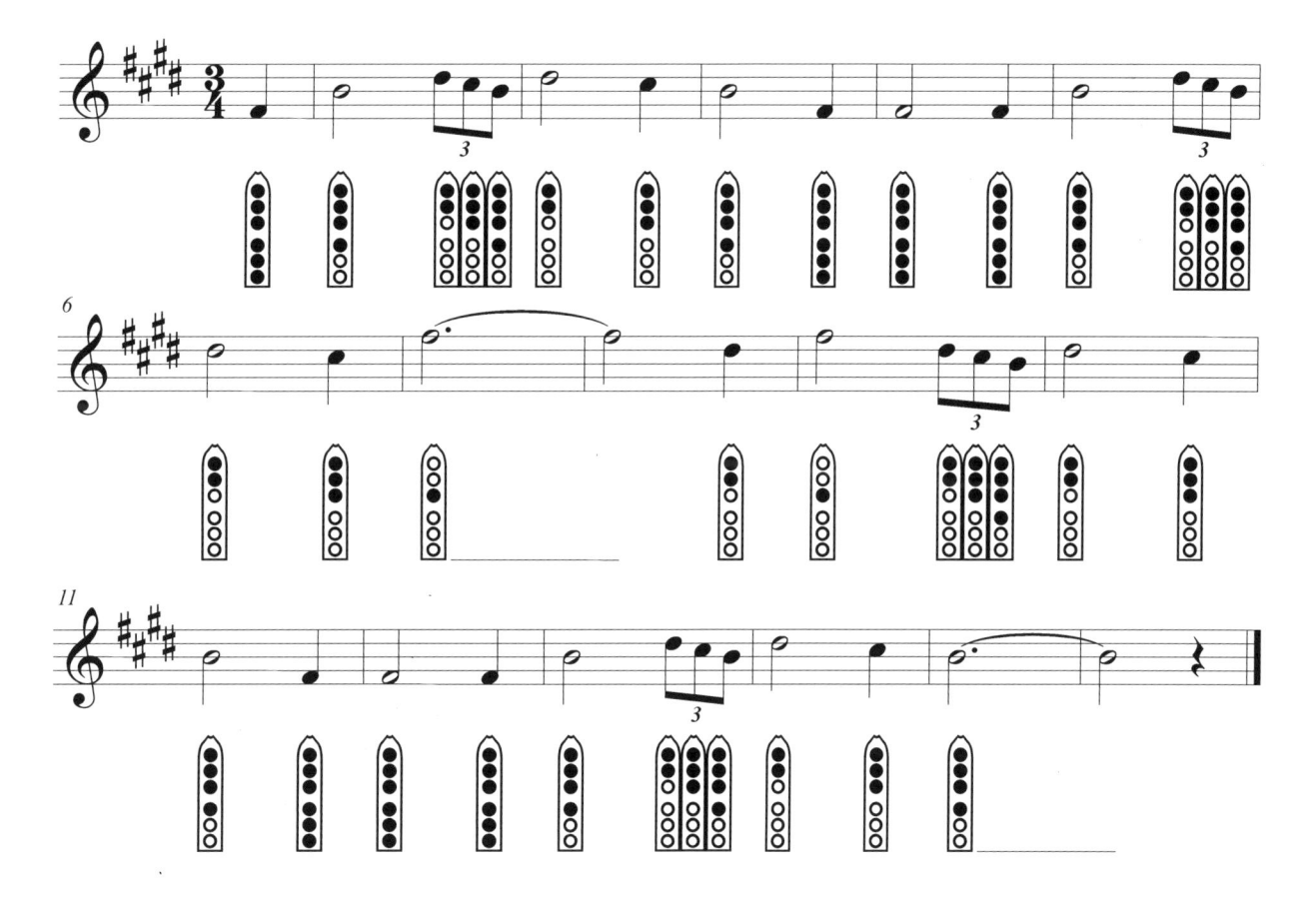

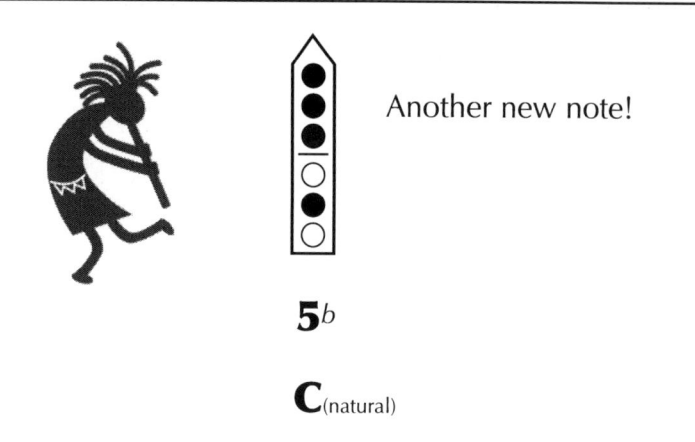

52 Learn to Play the Native American Style Flute with Ami Sarasvati

Another new note!

5♭

C(natural)

The Blues Scale

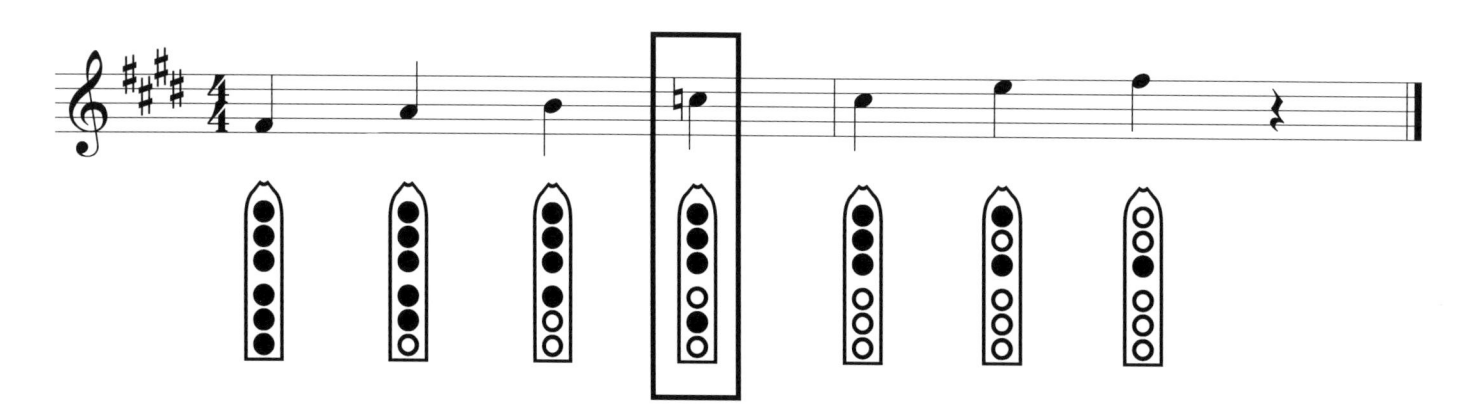

Notice that, when compared to the pentatonic scale, the Blues Scale has only one ADDITIONAL note placed right in the middle of the scale.

Blues Scale+

> Try this note too as an accent note!

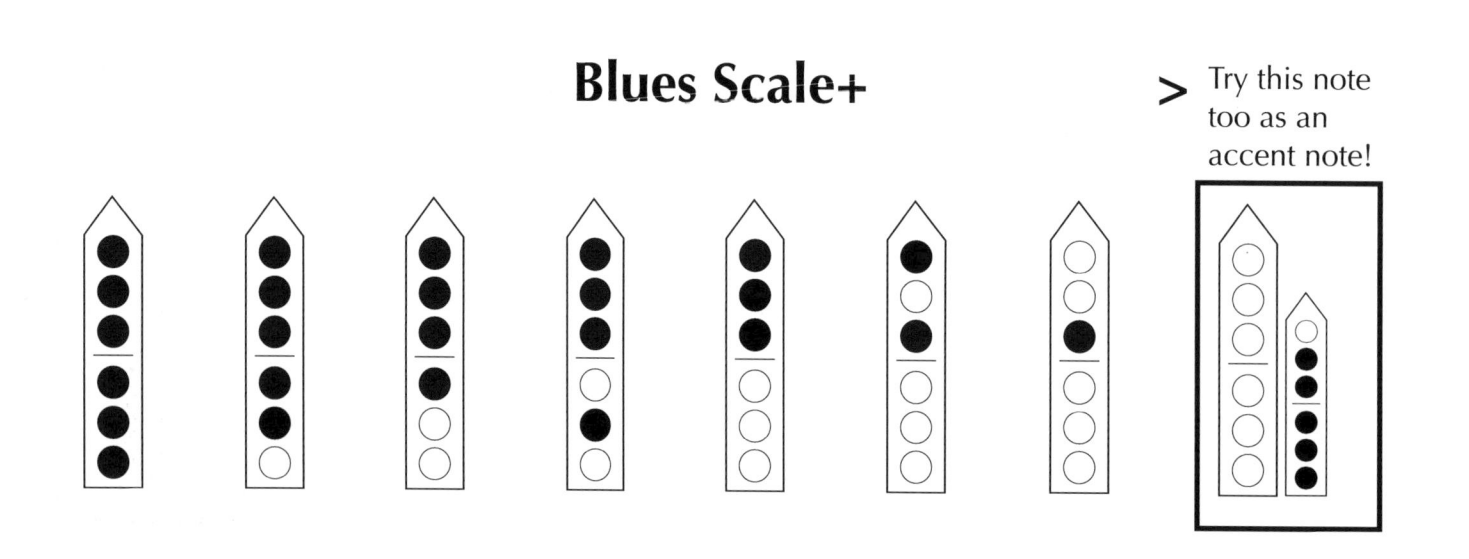

www.learntoplayNAF.com

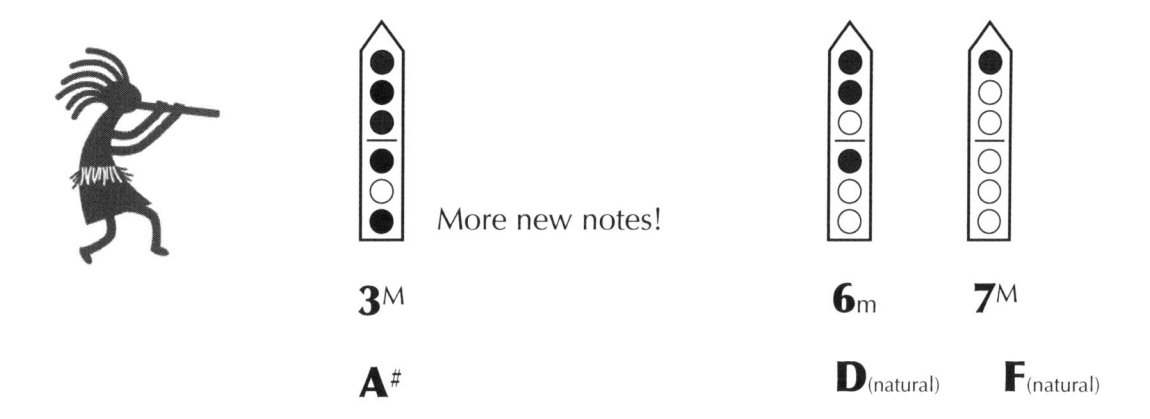

Learn to Play the Native American Style Flute with Ami Sarasvati   53

More new notes!

3M   **6**m   **7**M

A#   **D**(natural)   **F**(natural)

A Middle Eastern Scale

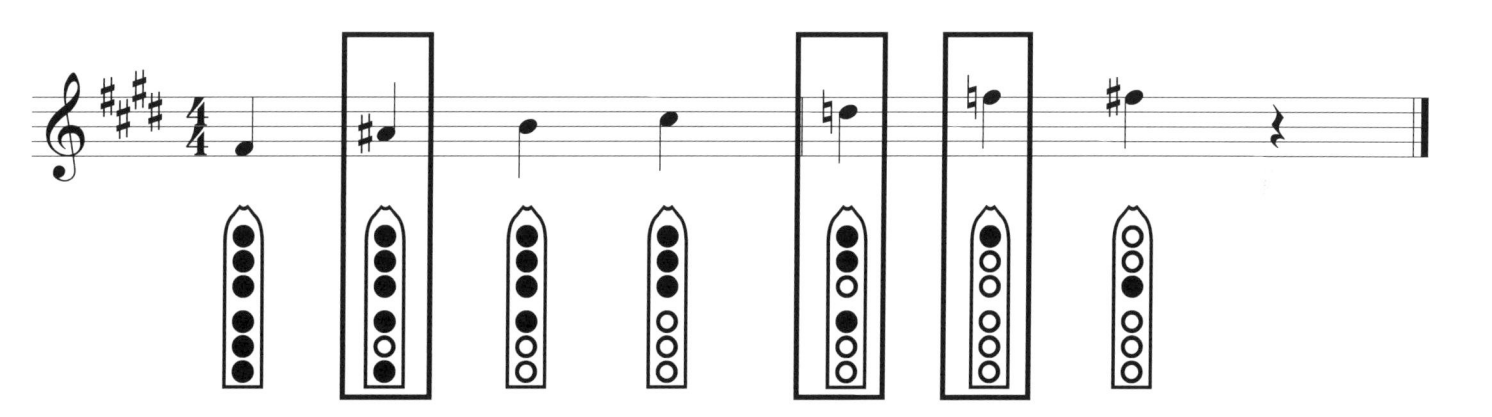

Here is a scale that create a mysterious and exotic sound.

Middle Eastern Scale +

> Try this note too as an accent note!

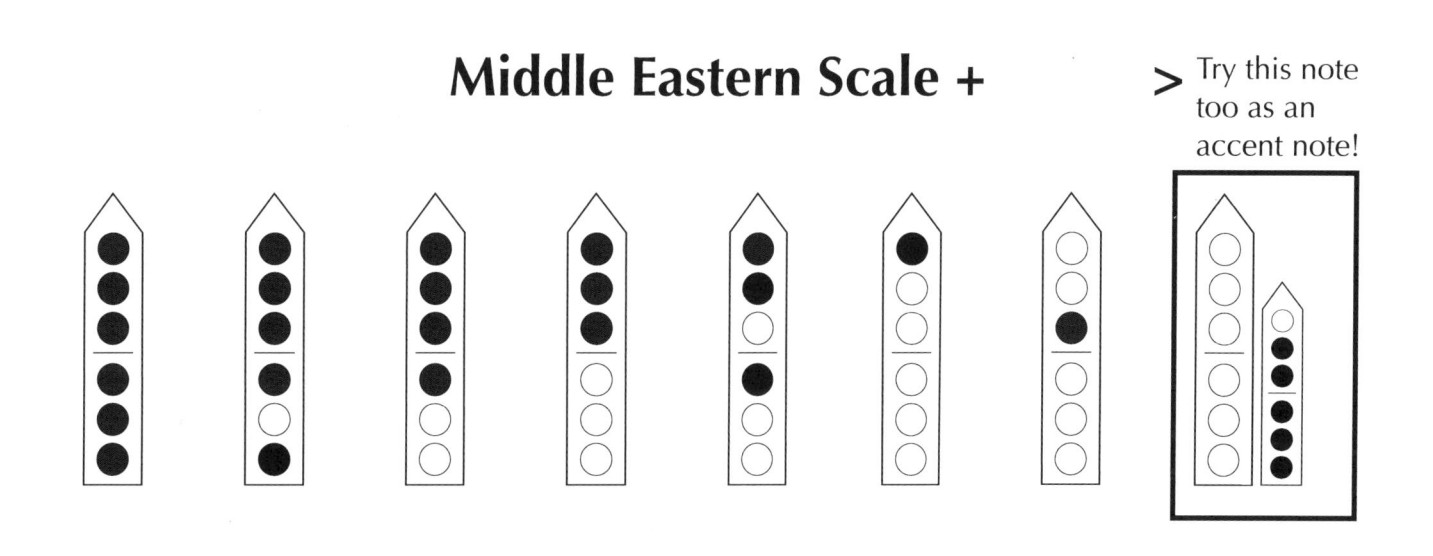

www.learntoplayNAF.com

Breath Phrasing Exercise

Use a pencil and place a comma to mark where you'd like to take breaths in this song. Breath phrasing is different for everyone. You don't need to totally run out of breath before taking a new one. Play the song and think about where it makes sense to take a new breath, paying attention to the musical phrasing. You can listen to this song on my SoundCloud recordings as well.

Kiowa Love Song

Traditional

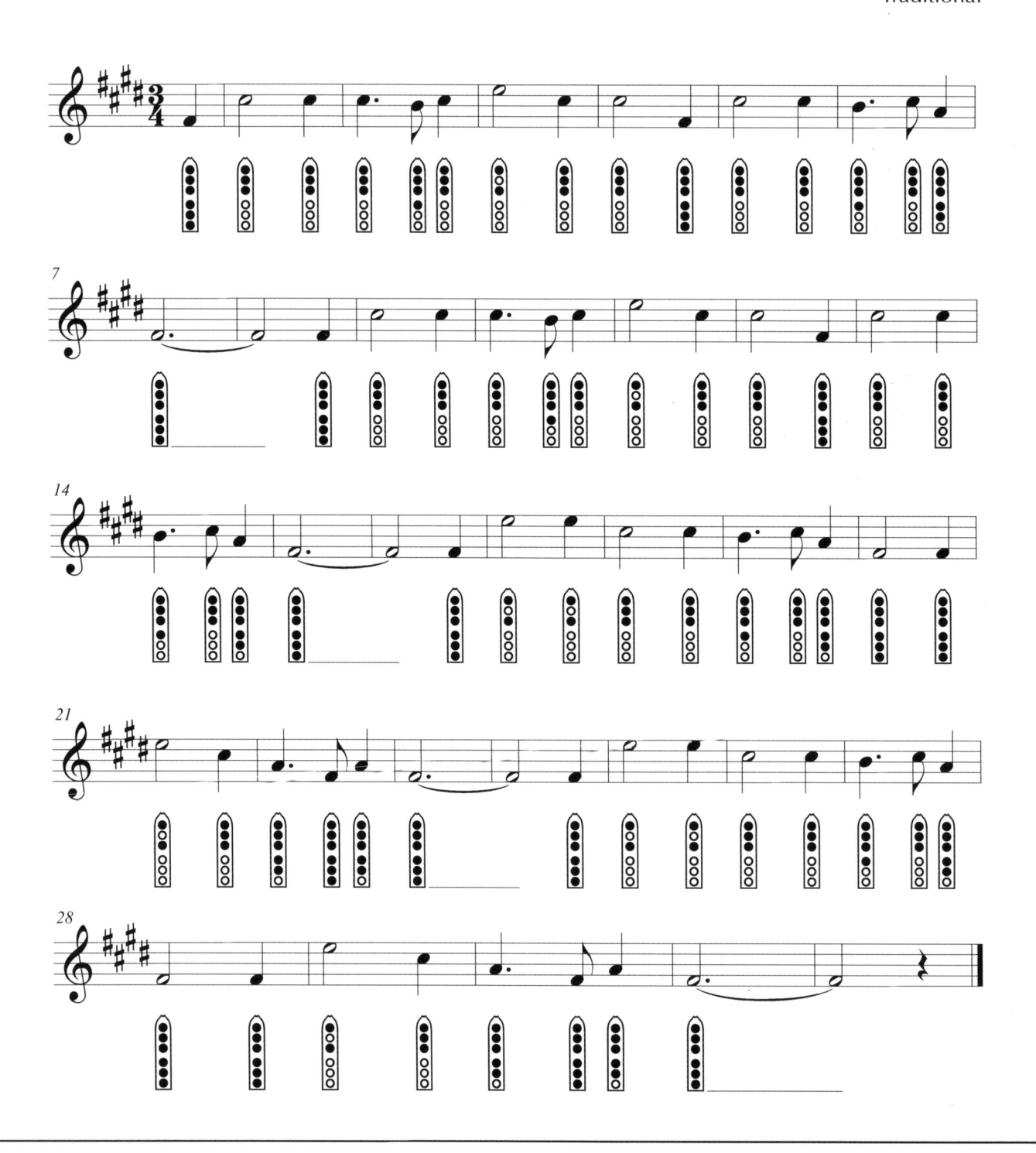

Anasazi Love Song
(for Native American flute)

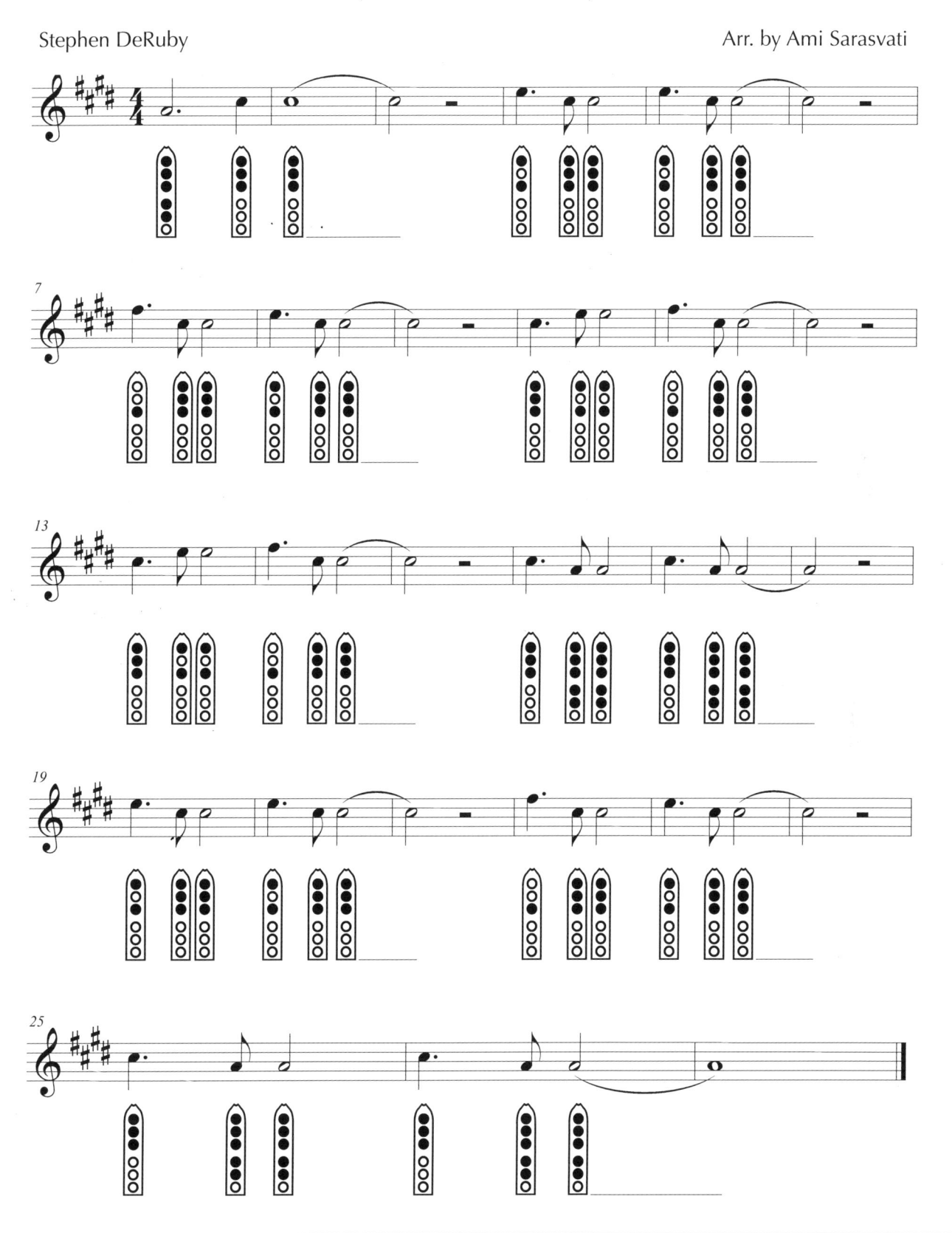

Stephen DeRuby

Arr. by Ami Sarasvati

Resources

Recommended Resources and Community:
- Flutopedia: www.flutopedia.com: an online encyclopedia for the Native American flute
- Flute School are amazing experiences all over the country each year: www.nativefluteschool.com
- World Flute Society membership and newsletter: www.worldflutesociety.org
- Clint Goss's newsletter: www.clintgoss.com/newsletter.html
- Flute Tree Foundation: www.flutetree.com
- Flute Portal: www.fluteportal.com a premier destination for information, discussion, and multimedia
- Facebook NAF groups
- Oregon Flute Store: books, CDs, flutes, cases, and many other NAF essentials www.oregonflutestore.com

Recommended Videos on the NAF:
- *Toubat, A Journey of the Native American Flute* available at www.oregonflutestore.com
- *SongKeepers* available at www.oregonflutestore.com

Recommended Flute Makers:
Please go to my website for the most current list and links of excellent flute makers: www.learntoplaynaf.com

Backing Tracks:
- Stephen DeRuby's CD, *Rhythms to Accompany the Native American Flute* available on Amazon
- Clint Goss's series *Jam Tracks for Native American Flute*: www.naftracks.com

Flute Circle Resources:
Flute Circle Facilitators Training: www.nativefluteschool.com

Recommended Flute Making Kit:
Northern Spirit Flutes
www.northernspiritflutes.net/ -- Note the ".net" at the end of this URL.
The Original Mid A Northern Spirit Flutes are available already made or in a kit. You can purchase the Build Kit which includes the tools you need to make the flutes (except for a power drill). These flutes are reliable, inexpensive, weather-proof, and make a perfect starter flute. I use them for starting students, flute circles, at workshops, and festivals. This is a turn-key solution for group NAF activities.

Music For People
www.musicforpeople.org
Music for People offers improvisational workshops and facilitator training for group music-making. Flute School by Clint Goss grew out of this outstanding and unique program.

NAF Daily Practice

Aim for 20 - 30 minutes play time.

Start with long tones. One long breath, one long note. Go up the pentatonic scale one note at a time.
Next, take a deep breath and slowly play up the whole scale in one breath, then another to come back down.

Dexterity Practice - 5 minutes and worth every second!

Exercise	Metronome
	1st time
	2nd time
	3rd time

Songs I'm working on:

Song	1st time BPM	2nd time BPM	Play without the metronome
Song	1st time BPM	2nd time BPM	Play without the metronome
Song	1st time BPM	2nd time BPM	Play without the metronome

***Now, put your book and metronome away
and simply play from the heart.***

NAF Weekly Practice

Aim for 20-30 minutes. Have your metronome, rhythm CD, flutes, and supplies on hand.	
Warm up (approx. 3 minutes)	• Long tones: take one long breath and play one long note. Go up the pentatonic scale one note at a time. Focus on your posture, relaxing your hands, and good tonal quality on each note. • Next, take a deep breath and play all the way up the scale in one breath, increasing the volume of breath as you ascend. Do this three times. Focus on efficiency of movement in your hands and keep your fingers close to the flute. • Finally, take a deep breath and play all the way down the scale in one breath, decreasing the volume of breath as you descend. Do this three times.

Dexterity Practice (approx. 5 minutes)	Exercise:	Metronome 1st time: ___ bpm
		Metronome 2nd time: ___ bpm
		Metronome 3rd time: ___ bpm

Songs this week		Metronome

Improvisation		

Memorizing		

Now, put your book and metronome away and simply play from the heart!

♥

Made in the USA
Middletown, DE
14 November 2021